YOUTH**WALK**™

Other Books in This Series

YOUTH**WALK** ™

Bruce H. Wilkinson
Executive Editor

Len Woods
Editor

Paula A. Kirk
General Editor

Walk Thru the Bible Ministries
Atlanta, Georgia

Zondervan Publishing House
Grand Rapids, Michigan

Youthwalk
Copyright © 1991 by Walk Thru the Bible Ministries
All rights reserved

Published by Zondervan Publishing House

Requests for information should be addressed to:
Walk Thru the Bible Ministries   or   Zondervan Publishing House
P.O. Box 80587   Grand Rapids, MI 49530
Atlanta, GA 30366

Library of Congress Cataloging-in-Publication Data

Youthwalk: sex, parents, popularity, and other topics for teen survival/
Walk Thru the Bible Ministries
   p. cm.
   Summary: A collection of daily devotional readings designed to highlight the grandeur of God's plan for humanity.
   ISBN 0-310-54231-6 (pbk.)
   1. Teenagers—Prayer-books and devotions—English. [1. Prayer books and devotions]. I. Walk Thru the Bible (Educational Ministry).
BV485.Y68   1991
242'.2—dc20   91—11979
                                              CIP
                                              AC

Cover and interior design by Michelle Beeman
Cover photo by Dan Stearns
Illustrations by AHA! Creative Solutions

Printed in the United States of America

94 95 96 97 98 99 00 01 02 / DH / 13 12 11 10 9 8 7 6 5

Dedication

Several years ago, God called us at Walk Thru the Bible to apply the lifechanging principles of His Word to the needs of youth, and *Youthwalk*, a practical Bible study guide for teens, was conceived. Then, because God provided encouragement and enablement through a precious Christian couple, the *Youthwalk* vision became a reality.

Stan and Alma Vermeer, themselves the parents of three dedicated Christian young people, immediately caught our vision. Having faithfully communicated the principles of God's Word to their own children, they knew that a dynamic relationship with Christ was the key to wholeness and hope for today's youth. Transforming their agreement with WTB's vision into action, Stan and Alma helped launch a spiritual resource that now has touched hundreds of thousands of young people across the nation.

Stan and Alma, we at Walk Thru the Bible lovingly and thankfully dedicate this volume to you, the godparents of *Youthwalk*. May God reward you with the knowledge that young lives have been changed forever as a result of your commitment to Him!

Bruce H. Wilkinson
Executive Editor

Acknowledgments

Youthwalk: Sex, Parents, Popularity, and Other Topics for Teen Survival is a fresh, new compilation of topical studies from *Youthwalk*, a magazine for teens published monthly by Walk Thru the Bible Ministries. We thank the many folks who have helped us out over the years, especially all the teens and youth leaders who made up our focus groups, posed for photos, and wrote articles and letters that kept us on the right track.

We're grateful too for the frequent contributions of Gene DiPaolo, Cary McNeal, and Dan Nelson. Their creativity has added greatly to both the art and editorial efforts.

Michelle Beeman, Kyle Henderson, Robyn Holmes, Kevin Johnson, and Stuart McLellan, our *Youthwalk* design and production team, have invested their time and talents to produce a book that will make a lasting difference in the lives of young people. From start to finish their concern and prayers have been with those who will read this book. Our special thanks go to them for their creative ideas and their perseverance in the production process.

Introduction

As a Christian teenager, are you sometimes confused by the modern world? Do you ever feel pressure to do things you know you shouldn't? Have you ever been asked a tough question about Christianity—and not known the answer? Are you ever embarrassed about sharing your faith?

If you answered any of those questions with a yes, I've got good news for you: you're not alone. But the book you have in your hand can help!

Youthwalk is carefully designed to help you understand the Bible and apply its truth to your life. *Youthwalk* will help you establish the Bible as your rock—your sure foundation in this unsure world. No longer will you see the Bible as a book of boring stories about things that happened eons ago. Instead, you'll see the Bible as *relevant*—a vital resource for you to live a happy, successful, and productive life.

We at Walk Thru the Bible Ministries are thrilled to join with Zondervan Publishing House to make this Bible-reading guide available to you.

Happy growing!

Bruce H. Wilkinson
President and Executive Editor
Walk Thru the Bible Ministries

How to Get the Most Out of *Youthwalk*

Youthwalk is arranged by topics—one for each week. You can start with the first topic or just jump in at any point in the book. Just put a check in the accompanying box to keep your place.

Each topic has an introductory page (to preview the topic) and five devotional pages (one for each weekday—Monday through Friday). Each of the daily devotional pages includes the following five sections:

1. *The Opening Story*—sets up the problem

2. *Look It Up*—shows what the Bible says about the problem

3. *Think It Through*—stimulates your thinking about the problem

4. *Work It Out*—gives practical suggestions for solving the problem

5. *Nail It Down*—shares other passages where you can find more wise counsel about the problem

6. *Pray About It*—lets you jot down prayer requests and praises

But that's not all! In addition to the weekly devotional topics, *Youthwalk* will educate, stimulate, and motivate you with these exciting features:

- *Hot Topic*—Each "Hot Topic" gives biblical answers to an important current issue.

- *Search for Satisfaction*—These pages are stories of humankind's ultimate search: a relationship with God through Jesus Christ.

- *Wide World of the Word*—These fun-filled pages are full of little-known facts about God's Word. Who said learning can't be enjoyable?

- *What on Earth Is God Like?*—These pages present the attributes of God in a down-to-earth way.

Do you want to do great things for God? Of course you do, or you wouldn't be reading this book. Follow the above instructions, and six months from now, you'll know God's Word better than you do today.

And that will be a great thing!

Walk Thru the Bible Ministries

Walk Thru the Bible Ministries (WTB) unofficially began in the early 1970s in Portland, Oregon, with the teaching of Old and New Testament surveys of the Bible. Dr. Bruce H. Wilkinson was looking for a way to innovatively teach the Word of God so that it would change people's lives.

Dr. Wilkinson officially founded WTB in 1976 as a nonprofit ministry. In 1978 WTB moved to its current home in Atlanta.

From these small beginnings WTB has grown into one of the leading Christian organizations in America with an international ministry extending to 21 countries in 30 languages. International branch offices are located in Australia, Brazil, Great Britain, Singapore, and New Zealand.

By focusing on the central themes of Scripture and their practical application to life, WTB has been able to develop and maintain wide acceptance in denominations and fellowships around the world. In addition, it has carefully initiated strategic ministry alliances with over one hundred Christian organizations and missions of wide diversity and background.

WTB has four major outreach ministries: seminars, publishing, leadership training, and video training.

The call of the Lord has been clear and consistent on Walk Thru the Bible as it strives to help fulfill the Lord's Great Commission. The highest ethics and standards of integrity are carefully practiced as Walk Thru the Bible lives out its commitment to excellence not only in ministry but also in its internal operational policies and procedures. No matter what the ministry, no matter where the ministry, WTB focuses on the Word of God and encourages people of all nations to grow in their knowledge of Him and in their unreserved obedience and service to Him.

CONTENTS

Topics

HOT TOPICS

WIDE WORLD OF THE WORD

THE SEARCH FOR SATISFACTION

WHAT ON EARTH IS GOD LIKE?

SECURITY
Getting rid of your blankets

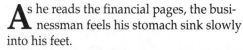

As he reads the financial pages, the businessman feels his stomach sink slowly into his feet.

The night before an important district game, the sophomore quarterback's heart is racing.

In the weeks leading up to the biggest dance of the year, several senior girls are frantically flirting and doing everything they can think of to get an invitation.

What these people need is a good dose of security!

"Surely he will never be shaken; a righteous man will be remembered forever. He will have no fear of bad new: his heart is steadfast, trusting in the LORD. His heart is secure, he will have no fear: in the end he will look in triumph on his foes" (Psalm 112:6-8).

Steve feels inse-cure. Oh, he doesn't walk around shivering and shaking. And he doesn't carry a blanket and suck his thumb. But sometimes he does feel uneasy when he thinks about all the horrible things going on in the world—abortion, racism, drugs, AIDS, violence, and environmental and natural disas-ters.

"It scares me to think what the world is going to be like in another 10 years," he gulps.

Uneasiness in an uncertain world

Look It Up: Everyone can relate (at one time or anoth-er) to the insecurity King David expressed in Psalm 55:

"My heart is in anguish within me; the terrors of death assail me. Fear and trembling have beset me; horror has overwhelmed me. I said, 'Oh, that I had the wings of a dove! I would fly away and be at rest—I would flee far away and stay in the desert; I would hurry to my place of shelter, far from the tempest and storm.'

"Confuse the wicked, O Lord, confound their speech, for I see violence and strife in the city. Day and night they prowl about on its walls; malice and abuse are within it. Destructive forces are at work in the city; threats and lies never leave its streets" (Psalm 55:4-11).

Think It Through: David wished he were a dove, able to fly out into the peaceful countryside. Have you ever felt like that? Where is the most peaceful place you've ever been? When have you felt the most secure?

What world (or personal) problems cause you to feel the most insecure?

Work It Out: Our goal this week is simple: to see what God says about finding security in a very insecure world. We need His help. So pray this way:

"Father, please speak to me. Give me open ears and a willing heart. As I read Your Word and spend time with You, slowly change my values. Help me begin to see things as You see them. And give me the deep confidence that comes from trusting You completely. Amen."

(Now go back and carefully reread the verse on the previous page.)

Nail It Down: Read a great description of the times in which we live—2 Timothy 3:1-5.

ONE SECURITY

In August Kay started going with Jerry. Handsome, funny, and athletic, Jerry was everything Kay ever dreamed of in a guy.

The problem is that without realizing it, Kay built her whole world around Jerry. For two months her whole self-worth was based on how he treated her. Compliments made her feel terrific. Criticism made her feel like scum.

This yo-yo lifestyle of security-insecurity hit rock bottom last night. Jerry suddenly cut the string. Kay is pretty much devastated . . . and feeling totally insecure.

Don't put your trust in people!

Look It Up: The Bible sternly warns us not to depend on other people to provide the security we crave.

• "Stop trusting in man, who has but a breath in his nostrils. Of what account is he?" (Isaiah 2:22).

• "This is what the LORD says: 'Cursed is the one who trusts in man, who depends on flesh for his strength and whose heart turns away from the LORD' " (Jeremiah 17:5).

Think It Through: Do you base your security on how others treat you? What's the danger in that kind of approach to life?

In a world of sinful people, is it realistic to expect to find anyone who will never let you down?

Work It Out: Take this quiz:
TRUE FALSE
____ ____ 1. It would destroy me if my friends suddenly blew me off.
____ ____ 2. I just can't stand it when I'm not going with someone.
____ ____ 3. What the kids at school think of me matters more than anything else.
____ ____ 4. I hate to be alone.
____ ____ 5. I am not happy unless I am together with my family and/or friends.
____ ____ 6. If someone close to me died or if my parents divorced, I don't think I'd want to live.

A "true" answer to any or all of those questions indicates that you may be depending on people for your security. Discuss the verses, the quiz, and the other ideas on this page with some mature Christian friends—and then pray for each other.

Nail It Down: Read Isaiah 31:1.

Pray About It:

TWO

Kenny's mom is out of work and she's worried about the family's lack of medical insurance. After hearing on the radio about some guy who won the lottery—$2.5 million a year for the next 20 years—Kenny lies back on the couch and starts fantasizing.

"Imagine that—$50 million! We could get the biggest house, the best cars, nice clothes—man, if we wanted, we could even hire our own personal doctor. Wouldn't that be great? Not a worry in the world. Set for life."

Stop counting (on) your money!

Look It Up: A lot of people think money is capable of solving all their problems. Wrong! Money can never bring security! Take it from these two very wealthy men:

Job—"If I have put my trust in gold or said to pure gold, 'You are my security,' if I have rejoiced over my great wealth, the fortune my hands had gained . . . then these also would be sins to be judged, for I would have been unfaithful to God on high" (Job 31:24-25, 28).

Solomon—"The wealth of the rich is their fortified city; they imagine it an unscalable wall" (Proverbs 18:11).

Think It Through: Are you counting on money to see you through life? Is having a certain lifestyle—and the money it will take to pay for it—the most important thing to you about your future?

Can you think of any ways that wealth is not as secure as it seems? How might it disappear quickly?

Work It Out: Fight the urge to look for security in money. Ron Blue, in his book *Master Your Money* (Thomas Nelson Publishers), gives three rules that will help you put money in the proper perspective:

"1. God owns it all.

"2. Money is never an end in itself, but is merely a resource used to accomplish other goals and obligations.

"3. Spend less than you earn and do it for a long time, and you will be financially successful."

Sounds simple, doesn't it? God's principle is faithfulness, not greed. If you're greedy, you'll eventually get burned (even if it takes a couple of generations). But if you're faithful, God will bless you, your children, and your grandchildren (Proverbs 13:22).

Nail It Down: Read Psalm 52:1-7 and 1 Timothy 6:17.

THREE SECURITY

Tammy comes home from school in tears. During sixth hour she found out her "friends" have been spreading a very vicious rumor about her. Talk about embarrassed!

"I'll never be able to show my face there ever again," she sobs. Mr. Krauss puts his arms around his daughter, pulls her close, and gives her a long hug.

"Sweetie, I'm so sorry. I know it doesn't change your situation, but . . . I love you."

"Thanks, Dad," Tammy sniffles.

Seeking out the source of security

Look It Up: Isn't it great to have an earthly dad who cares? Isn't it even greater to have a heavenly Father who cares perfectly and all the time?

• "I have set the LORD always before me. Because he is at my right hand, I will not be shaken" (Psalm 16:8).

• "For the king trusts in the LORD; through the unfailing love of the Most High he will not be shaken" (Psalm 21:7).

• "So we say with confidence, 'The Lord is my helper; I will not be afraid. What can man do to me?' "(Hebrews 13:6).

Do you see the common thread that runs through these passages? It's this: The source of ultimate security is the Lord our God!

Think It Through: It's okay to go to friends and/or family members with your problems. But remember this: People will eventually let you down. They have bad days and problems of their own. If your trust is in them alone, you'll definitely be disappointed.

Look first to the Lord. With Him as your security, you won't fall apart when your world does.

Work It Out: People look for security in all kinds of places—romantic relationships, a high grade point average, a close family, a good job, a promising future, a special talent or natural ability, a group of friends, a certain routine, good looks, and material possessions.

List the potential problems that face people who make one of the above the basis for their security. If you sense that you are trusting in one of those things more than you are the Lord, ask God to show you how to change.

Nail It Down: Read Psalm 55:22.

Pray About It:

FOUR

17

Mark just knew he was going to make first string on the football team. He made sure his parents, girlfriend, and other classmates knew it too. Imagine Mark's surprise (and embarrassment) when he didn't start. (He only played about 10 plays in the first two games!)

Martha has felt panicky and uptight for three weeks now. She and her boyfriend went all the way. She's terribly afraid she might be pregnant.

Installing your own security system

Look It Up: Our actions often determine whether we are secure or insecure. We find security when we
• obey Christ—"Therefore everyone who hears these words of mine and puts them into practice is like a wise man who built his house on the rock. The rain came down, the streams rose, and the winds blew and beat against that house; yet it did not fall, because it had its foundation on the rock" (Matthew 7:24-25);
• live wisely—"He who trusts in himself is a fool, but he who walks in wisdom is kept safe" (Proverbs 28:26).
But we experience insecurity when we
• are proud—"So, if you think you are standing firm, be careful that you don't fall!"—(1 Corinthians 10:12);
• are disobedient to God—(Matthew 7:26-27).

Think It Through: What could Mark and Martha have done to prevent the insecurity they now feel?

Work It Out: Install your own security system.
1. Obey God's Word. (The commands that seem so negative—no sex, no partying, no filthy talk, no cheating—are actually positive. Following them builds security!)
2. Hang around people who want to live for God. (Rebellious, insecure people want to drag you down. Misery loves company, right?)
3. Seek to know Jesus Christ. (He loves and accepts you totally and completely. He'll never reject you. You can count on Him!)

Nail It Down: Read how pride brought destruction (and ultimate insecurity) to Edom—Obadiah 3-4. On Saturday, read Psalm 46. On Sunday, read more about the ultimate source of security and help— Psalm 40.

FIVE SECURITY

···TEMPTATION···

Saying no to Satan's schemes

Some people are out looking for trouble—and finding it with amazing success!

Not you. The fact that you're reading this book means you're different. You want to live for God.

You want to overcome the tempting situations in your life. And you'd probably like some help.

Well, you've come to the right place! Our goal this week is to understand temptation better so that we might learn how to say no to the seductive scheme of the evil one.

" . . . in order that Satan might not outwit us. For we are not unaware of his schemes" (2 Corinthians 2:11).

Anatomy of a seduction

Look It Up: A classic example of temptation is King David's downward slide into adultery and murder.

"In the spring, at the time when kings go off to war, David sent Joab out with . . . the whole Israelite army. . . But David remained in Jerusalem.

"One evening David got up from his bed and walked around on the roof of the palace. From the roof he saw a woman bathing. The woman was very beautiful, and David sent someone to find out about her" (2 Samuel 11:1-3).

The next verse says that "David sent messengers to get her. She came to him, and he slept with her" (v. 4). Maybe you know the rest of the story. The woman, Bathsheba, ended up pregnant, and David had her husband killed to cover his sin.

Think It Through: Do you think David consciously thought: "I know what! I'll spend tonight with Uriah's wife! For a few hours of pleasure, I'll ruin my life. Yep, that's what I want to accomplish today!"?

Of course not! No one purposely plans to wreck his life! But think it through: If a godly person like David could so easily yield to temptation, what should that say to you and me?

Work It Out: Learn from David's mistakes.
1. Be where you're supposed to be! (Had David been with his troops, he wouldn't have sinned.)
2. Don't be idle! (By lazing around with nothing to do, David was a prime candidate for a big fall.)
3. At the first sign of trouble, run! (David stopped and stared.)
4. Don't entertain thoughts of sin! (As soon as David inquired about Bathsheba, his goose was cooked. The only thing left was to send for her.)

Nail It Down: Read James 1:14-15.

TEMPTATION

ONE

Patti (a sophomore who struggles with bulimia) moans, "Why does God keep tempting me like this?" as she stares at all the junk food on her friend's counter.

• After going too far with his girlfriend (again!), Michael tries to ease his guilty conscience: "If only Kate wasn't so beautiful," he rationalizes. "The way she looks at me, the way she dresses—it's all her fault!"

Who's giving the orders?

Look It Up: Let's look at each of those excuses in light of God's Word:

First, the idea that God is the source of temptation. "When tempted, no one should say, 'God is tempting me.' For God cannot be tempted by evil, nor does he tempt anyone" (James 1:13).

Second, that others are the source of temptation. "He [Jesus] spoke plainly about this [His arrest, crucifixion, and resurrection], and Peter took him aside and began to rebuke him.

"But when Jesus turned . . . he rebuked Peter. 'Get behind me, Satan!' he said" (Mark 8:32-33).

Think It Through: Jesus' reaction to Peter is interesting. It tells us that Satan is the ultimate source of the temptations in our lives. God is involved in the sense that He allows us to undergo temptation. And people are involved in the sense that Satan uses them to tempt us to do evil. But the real tempter is the devil himself.

In what ways has Satan recently been using people to tempt you to do wrong things?

Work It Out: Have you been blaming God or other people for the temptations in your life? Remember that people are not ultimately responsible. The engineer behind it all is the devil himself. Pray this:

"Father in heaven, I am constantly tempted from every side. Thank You for showing me who the real culprit is. Help me not to take the devil lightly. Give me wisdom to know how to fight back. And give me the desire to say no to the devil's schemes. Thank You. In Jesus' name. Amen."

Nail It Down: Find out more about Satan, the master tempter. Read 1 Chronicles 21:1; 2 Corinthians 11:3; and 1 Thessalonians 3:5.

Pray About It:

TWO

■ ■ ■ ■ ■

A junior in high school, Anna received a credit card application in the mail. Figuring, "What difference does it make— maybe they'll actually give me one," she requested a card with her name on it.

Would you believe she got a card? And would you believe that in six weeks, she's already run up a bill of $565!

"My parents are going to kill me! But, it's like every time I go to the mall, I see all these things I want, and I can't seem to say no."

Sending the serpent on his way

Look It Up: *Question:* How can we overcome temptation (whether it's to spend too much money, get sexually involved, cheat at school, eat too much, or go where we shouldn't)? *Answer:* By following the example of Jesus.

Led into the wilderness, the Son of God was subjected to a variety of temptations. And each time Christ resisted enticements to sin by quoting Scripture. Finally He said:

"'Away from me, Satan! For it is written: "Worship the Lord your God, and serve him only."'

"Then the devil left him, and angels came and attended him." (Matthew 4:10-11).

Think It Through: Get rid of the notion that the devil can make you sin. (As we saw yesterday, Satan is the source of temptation, the one who constantly dangles tantalizing offers in front of us. However, we always have a choice about whether or not we will sin.)

When we yield to temptation, we can't blame God, our friends, or even the devil. The fault is ours!

Work It Out: Jesus quoted Scripture as a defense against temptation. Regardless of feelings or circumstances, He kept coming back to the fact of God's Word. Every time the tempter opened his mouth, Jesus responded, "It is written . . . "

That's a good example to follow—quoting Bible verses in the heat of spiritual battles. So memorize a couple of verses today that deal with the specific temptations you face.

Then, for fun, listen to the innovative song "Dust Man" on Morgan Cryar's album "Like a River" (Reunion Records).

Nail It Down: Read the encouraging promise in James 4:7 (and claim it all through the day)!

······ THREE TEMPTATION ··

Janie's idea of heaven would be a sunny place with plenty of open road where she could put on her shades, pop the top on her very own Volkswagen convertible, crank up the stereo, and drive to her heart's content. More than anything, she loves to drive.

Problem is, Janie's only 14. So how does she know how much fun driving is? Answer: She sneaks the car out when her parents are gone! The minute they leave, the tempter shows up: "Go for it, Janie! Now's your chance!"

Janie seems powerless to say no.

Becoming an overcomer

Look It Up: How can Janie (or anyone) become an overcomer when temptation strikes?

1. By remembering the command of God: "Do not offer the parts of your body to sin, as instruments of wickedness, but rather offer yourselves to God, as those who have been brought from death to life; and offer the parts of your body to him as instruments of righteousness" (Romans 6:13).

2. By remembering the promise of God: "No temptation has seized you except what is common to man. And God is faithful; he will not let you be tempted beyond what you can bear. But when you are tempted, he will also provide a way out so that you can stand up under it" (1 Corinthians 10:13).

Think It Through: How would you advise Janie?

Is there a particular area in your life where, like Janie, you seem to be especially susceptible to temptation?

What advice would you give to someone who is facing a problem exactly like yours? (Why not take your own advice?)

Work It Out: Today when temptation strikes (and it will, unless you're dead!), remember:

• Others are facing a similar temptation. (Band together and draw strength from each other!)

• God won't let the temptation become unbearable. (No matter how you feel, you can resist!)

• God will provide a way out. (Look for an escape hatch!)

If you want to really come to grips with the issue of temptation, read the superb book, *Temptation,* by Charles Stanley (Oliver Nelson Publishers).

Nail It Down: Read Proverbs 1:10.

Pray About It:

FOUR

23

Keith, 15, has a problem with lust.

As a Christian, he feels really guilty when he yields to this temptation, reads *Playboy*, and masturbates. He's prayed about his problem, has read everything he can find on the topic, and has seriously vowed to stop; but nothing seems to work.

"What can I do to make the temptation to lust go away?"

The good news about temptation

Look It Up: The bad news is that, in this life, we will always face temptation. The good news is that we can avoid some temptations, and we can flee all the rest.

Remember Joseph? When his master's wife begged him to sleep with her, notice his reaction:

"And though she spoke to Joseph day after day, he refused to go to bed with her or even be with her.

"One day he went into the house to attend to his duties, and none of the household servants was inside. She caught him by his cloak and said, 'Come to bed with me!' But he left his cloak in her hand and ran out of the house" (Genesis 39:10-12).

Think It Through: As much as possible, Joseph avoided his master's wife. And when she cornered him, he literally ran away!

Why is it important to stop temptations in their tracks? Because temptations are like stray cats—feed one, and he'll soon return with all his friends!

When you're in a potentially dangerous situation, do you do your best to flee (2 Timothy 2:22)?

Work It Out: If you are tempted to:
• Lust—avoid certain movies, magazines, and TV shows.
• Be sexually involved—go on group dates and avoid dark, secluded places.
• Cheat at school—study hard, and then sit alone.
• Drink—stay away from parties and other places where alcohol is served.
• Be materialistic—don't go to the mall. (Part of the solution to temptation is using common sense!)

Nail It Down: On Saturday, see the wrong way to respond to temptation in Proverbs 7:6-27. Then on Sunday, reflect on the right response to temptation— 2 Kings 5:16.

FIVE **TEMPTATION·**

··COMPETITION·*·*·*
The truth about winning & losing

No honest person would deny having, at least in certain areas of life, a deep-seated urge to come out on top. And no thinking person would deny that a win-at-all-costs attitude pervades our society.

But is competition right? What about the unsportsmanlike behavior on the athletic field? . . . the fight for attention at home? . . . the cut-throat mentality in the classroom? . . . the petty rivalries between churches? . . . the backstabbing between friends?

"For my thoughts are not your thoughts, neither are your ways my ways, declares the LORD" (Isaiah 55:8).

Since the age of 5, Sandy has been playing golf. Lessons, daily practice, tournaments—the fact is, Sandy's whole life is golf. Or maybe we should say, winning at golf. (His father hopes he'll be a pro one day!)

Sandy is so obsessed with being the best, he cheats on his score, curses and scatters clubs after each bad shot, and gloats whenever he beats an opponent. No wonder no one wants to play with him!

Having fun at fun and games

Look It Up: The Bible provides wisdom and warnings about taking sports too seriously:

1. Our worth as individuals is based on who we are (Genesis 1:27; Colossians 3:12), not how well we do.

2. Athletic prowess has very limited, short-term value (1 Timothy 4:8). What good is winning a game if, in the process, you're a rotten friend and an inconsistent Christian?

3. Jesus Christ, not winning, must be first in our lives. "And he is the head of the body, the church; he is the beginning and the firstborn from among the dead, so that in everything he might have the supremacy" (Colossians 1:18).

Think It Through: Whatever happened to fun in sports? Little kids, just learning how to play soccer, have a blast running around, being with their friends, falling down, laughing together. Then we adults come along and introduce them to the win-lose trap.

Almost immediately the joy is gone. The game becomes a contest, the score becomes all-important, and the opponents become the enemy.

Work It Out: Fight the win-at-all-costs mentality.
• Don't keep score next time you play a game.
• Switch your goal from "beating the other guy" to making a good shot, executing a good pass, or improving your technique.
• If you can't seem to participate in certain activities without getting heated and intense, lay off those activities for a few weeks.
• Most important, ask God to change your desires and attitudes. Ask Him to teach you to play with fun, not the final outcome, on your mind.

Nail It Down: Read about the danger of gloating over a fallen opponent—Proverbs 24:17-18.

★ ★ ★ ★ ★ ★ ONE COMPETITION

As Kent, 17, walks past his younger brother's room, he hears the sounds of muffled sobs.

After 10 minutes of banging on the door and 10 more minutes of "C'mon, Scooter, what's wrong?" he finally gets this confession:

"Mom and Dad never jump on your case. Everything you do is 'perfect' and 'wonderful.' Meanwhile, I can't do anything right! I bet Dad asks me 50 times a week, 'Why can't you be more like Kent?' "

Competition . . . relatively speaking

Look It Up: Competing for love and approval. Many of us do it—consciously or unconsciously—all the time. Here are two examples:

1. The story of the brothers Jacob and Esau:

"When Esau heard his father's words [that Jacob had been given a special blessing], he burst out with a loud and bitter cry and said to his father, 'Bless me—me too, my father! . . . Haven't you reserved any blessing for me?' . . . Then Esau wept aloud" (Genesis 27:34, 36, 38).

2. The story of the Prodigal Son (Luke 15:11-32).

Think It Through: Do you compete with your brother(s) and/or sister(s) for your parents' love and favor? What strategies do you use to try to get attention?

Is it right for parents to play favorites? Why or why not? How does that make you feel? Would your family be better if this competition ended?

Work It Out: The problem with competition (especially the rivalries between brothers and sisters) is that it results in winners and losers. If you lose, you feel awful. If you win, others feel awful. So no matter what, someone ends up hurt.

If your parents treat you specially, try deflecting some of that attention to your siblings. Brag about them to your parents. Point out the good things they have done. If the special treatment continues, talk to your parents and express your concern.

If you are the one who feels overshadowed and forgotten, tell God and another friend about your hurt feelings. Then prayerfully approach your parents about the issue.

Nail It Down: Read another account of sibling rivalry —Genesis 37:1-4.

Pray About It:

★ ★ ★ ★ ★ TWO

27

M arianne makes straight A's. She's intelligent, she knows it, and she lets everyone else know it! Her goal is to be the valedictorian of the senior class.

Trouble is, David is equally smart. And he is also determined to graduate number one.

What a fierce competition! The two students keeping track of each other's GPAs . . . freaking out over every missed bonus question . . . rejoicing over each slip by the "enemy."

Crunch time in the classroom

Look It Up: It has nothing to do with grades, but this Biblical reference to Satan illustrates that pride is often the motivation behind our desire to be number one:

"You said in your heart, 'I will ascend to heaven; I will raise my throne above the stars of God; I will sit enthroned on the mount of assembly, on the utmost heights of the sacred mountain. I will ascend above the tops of the clouds; I will make myself like the Most High'" (Isaiah 14:13-14).

Perhaps it was thinking on this verse that prompted C. S. Lewis to write in *Mere Christianity:* "The essential vice, the utmost evil, is pride . . . It was through pride that the devil became the devil: pride leads to every other vice; it is the complete anti-God state of mind."

Think It Through: Lewis continues with this insightful comment:

"Pride is essentially competitive—is competitive by its very nature. Pride gets no pleasure out of having something, only out of having more of it than the next man. . . It is the comparison that makes you proud: the pleasure of being above the rest."

Are you prideful when it comes to grades? In other areas of life?

Work It Out: First, ask God to change your attitude from "I have to be the best" to "I want to do my best."

Second, seek to avoid finding out the grades—or salaries or test scores—others receive. (What's the point? If you do better, you'll be prideful; if you do worse, you'll feel stupid!)

Third, let your goal in school be learning, not grades.

Nail It Down: Read about how God resists the proud —Proverbs 3:34; James 4:6; and 1 Peter 5:5-7.

* * * * * * **THREE** **COMPETITION**

Church A and church B are not only in the same neighborhood, they're also part of the same religious denomination. You might expect them to work together on projects.

Well, think again. The truth is that the two churches act as if they're mortal enemies! If A launches a new ministry, B follows suit. If the youth group at B plans an event, the staff at A schedules something even bigger!

But we're on the same team

Look It Up: Hey, Christians! We are not in competition with each other. And we never have been. See?

"For when one says, 'I follow Paul,' and another, 'I follow Apollos,' are you not mere men?

"What, after all, is Apollos? And what is Paul? Only servants, through whom you came to believe— as the Lord has assigned each his task. I planted the seed, Apollos watered it, but God made it grow. So neither he who plants nor he who waters is anything, but only God, who makes things grow. . . . For we are God's fellow workers" (1 Corinthians 3:4-7, 9).

Think It Through: During the night the parts of your body quit cooperating. Each nerve decides, "I want all the attention on me!" Suddenly your whole body is wide awake, screaming with pain.

Then your heart turns to your eyes and says, "I bet I can beat faster than you can blink." And off they go!

With every part doing its own thing, your body is soon in total chaos! You're incapable of functioning.

That's how it is when members of the body of Christ compete instead of cooperate.

Work It Out: Work to create a spirit of cooperation among your Christian friends:
• Pray for unity (John 17:22-23).
• Reject the temptation to bad-mouth other believers or churches (1 Timothy 5:13).
• Reread Paul's words in 1 Corinthians 3, and note that the focus and goals of all Christians should be the same—bringing glory to God, not to ourselves.

Nail It Down: Notice that dissension and jealousy (in other words, competition) are included in a list of very undesirable kinds of behaviors—Romans 13:13.

Pray About It:

★ ★ ★ ★ ★ FOUR

Mark is angry. Here's why: Two weeks ago he met Heather, a new girl at church. He talked to her for five minutes, and he was hooked!

Immediately he found his best friend, Terry, and told him everything. "She's awesome! I'm calling her tonight for next weekend."

Sure enough, Heather was interested, but had to go out of town.

When Mark called again, Heather replied, "I'd love to Mark, but I'm already going snowboarding with Terry."

Now do you see why Mark is so hurt and angry?

With friends like these . . .

Look It Up: Let's look at some rules that can help reduce the competition between friends:
- The Golden Rule—"Do to others as you would have them do to you" (Luke 6:31).
- The Love Rule—"Love does no harm to its neighbor. Therefore love is the fulfillment of the law" (Romans 13:10).
- The Rule of Unselfishness—"Nobody should seek his own good, but the good of others" (1 Corinthians 10:24).

Follow those rules and your friendships can't help but get better!

Think It Through: Have you ever pulled a stunt like the one Terry pulled on Mark? What happened?

How would you feel if you were in Mark's shoes? What should Mark do in response? Anything?

Work It Out: List the competitive situations you face with your closest friends (vying for the same honor, award, position on the team, elective office, boyfriend/girlfriend, etc.).

Realize this—you can either let those things come between you . . . or you can apply the friendship rules listed in "Look It Up."

Say, "The Golden Rule demands that I _____ in this situation." (Be specific!) Do this with each rule . . . and for each potential problem area.

Nail It Down: On Saturday, consider how Abraham sought to avoid competing with Lot—Genesis 13: 5-12. On Sunday, compare Christ's spirit of humility to the spirit of competition which pervades our society—2 Corinthians 8:9.

★ ★ ★ ★ ★ ★ F I V E **COMPETITION**

DIVORCE

O nce upon a time . . . divorce was a dirty word. It was scandalous—
something done in secret, in Hollywood maybe. Not any more.
Now over half of the people who marry will eventually divorce. What in
the world is happening?

Not God's Ideal. The Bible condemns divorce in the strongest possible
terms: "'*I hate divorce,' says the LORD God of Israel*" (Malachi 2:16).

It has always been God's plan for married couples to stay together till
death. This is because when a man and woman join themselves in marriage, they are bonded together in a unique way (Genesis 2:24). Jesus
noted this and added, "*What God has joined together, let man not separate*"
(Matthew 19:6).

Clearly, divorce is not part of God's intended plan. Though He has
permitted it under rare circumstances (Ezra 9,10), it is never an act that
brings glory to Him or happiness to the couple.

Different Views. Christians are sharply divided over the divorce issue.
Some, citing Jesus' words above, believe that divorce is wrong in all cases.
These believers might allow a *temporary* separation for the purpose of
working out problems, but would not see divorce as an option.

Another viewpoint argues that divorce, while never *desirable*, is *allow-
able* when sexual immorality has disrupted the marriage relationship.
This position is based on Jesus' statement in Matthew 19:9: "*I tell you
that anyone who divorces his wife, except for marital unfaithfulness and marries
another woman commits adultery.*"

Still others offer even less strict interpretations.

Steps to Take. Few issues are as complicated as divorce. Perhaps you
live in a home that has felt the pain of a failed marriage. Maybe you
have friends in that situation. Whatever the case, do these things:

• Study Matthew 5:32; 1 Corinthians 7:10–15; and Ephesians 5:22–33.
Determine if divorce is ever acceptable for a Christian.

• Be reminded of God's faithfulness and love during painful family
times (Psalm 30).

• Do some reading about how to deal with conflict, what to look for
in a partner, and how to build strong relationships.

• Ask God for His amazing grace, so that if you marry in a world that has
forgotten what it means to be committed, you will stay married for good.

It's no guarantee, but that's your best bet to finding a relationship
where you'll . . . live happily ever after.

A CONVERSATION
ABOUT LIFE

What are you gonna do after you graduate?
Go to college and party—and get a degree.

What about after that?
I dunno. Get a job where I can make lots of money.

And then?
Well, settle down—get married, buy a house, have kids.

And after that?
You mean after the kids grow up?

Yeah.
I guess I'll retire.

And do what?
Gosh, I don't know . . . get old and play bingo. Travel. That's a long time from now.

And then?
What do you mean?

I mean what'll you do after you're old?
Well . . . I guess I . . . you know what I'll do. I'll get old and die just like everybody else.

And then what?

Only a really strange person sits around thinking about death all the time. But only a fool goes through life without thinking about death. Here's what the Bible says about life now and later:

"God has given us eternal life, and this life is in his Son. He who has the Son has life; He who does not have the Son of God does not have life" (1 John 5:11-12).

The message is clear: Without Christ there's no life. Not here. Not ever.

If you haven't trusted Him as your Savior, do so today. You'll get a purpose for living and the promise of heaven.

Who says nothing's free anymore?

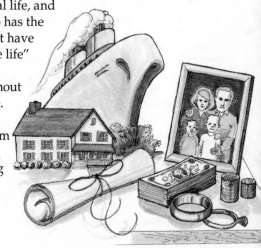

***** DRUGS ********
So long to substance abuse

Everybody—doctors, politicians, psychologists, parents, educators, journalists—has an idea for coping with the drug crisis.

Some call for better education; others scream for tougher law enforcement.

The bottom line? We are spending more and more money on a problem that continues to get worse and worse.

Don't you think it's time we looked at (and listened to) what God says?

"Show me your ways, O LORD, teach me your paths; guide me in your truth and teach me, for you are God my Savior, and my hope is in you all day long" (Psalm 25:4-5).

* *

Walk into certain restrooms at H. B. Devlin Senior High School, and you'll practically choke on the acrid smell of pot smoke.

Hang out behind the gym after school and you can score cocaine, crack, or any of the latest designer drugs.

Drop by one of the weekend parties and you can drop acid or PCP—that is, if you get there before the supply runs out.

Users, abusers, and other losers

Look It Up: The Bible doesn't mention marijuana, crack, acid, PCP, or designer drugs. Nevertheless, there are indications that drug abuse is not new.

The Greek word which is translated "magic arts" in Revelation 9:21 is *pharmakeia*, the same word from which we get our word *pharmacy*. (See also sorceries in Isaiah 47:9 and 12.) These magic arts and sorceries often involved the use of some form of drugs to contact demonic forces.

Elsewhere, the same Greek word is translated "witchcraft" and is found in a list of activities which God hates. "The acts of the sinful nature are obvious: sexual immorality, impurity and debauchery; idolatry and witchcraft; hatred, discord, jealousy, fits of rage, selfish ambition, dissensions, factions and envy; drunkenness, orgies" (Galatians 5:19-21).

Think It Through: The statistics vary, but even the most encouraging, most recent survey of the National Parents' Resource Institute for Drug Education (PRIDE) contains bad news:

• Twenty-four percent of teens regularly drink.
• Eleven percent of teenagers smoke marijuana.
• Two percent of high school students use cocaine at least once a month.

Substance abuse is a serious problem.

How bad is the problem in your community?

Work It Out: Look again at the list of sins in Galatians 5:19-21. How many of those activities are often associated with drug abuse? If you don't know much about illegal drugs and their effects, go to your school or public library and become informed.

Nail It Down: See the alternative to a life of substance abuse— Galatians 5:22-25.

*******  ONE DRUGS **********

We asked some of the users at H. B. Devlin High, "Why do you get high?" Here's what they said:

Ken: "It's a form of amusement. Drugs feel good."

Gina: "Drugs cover up the pain. They take away the depression . . . except that after awhile, you have to keep using them just to feel normal."

Michelle: "It's the peer pressure. You've got all your friends telling you, 'C'mon, be cool!' It seems no different from my dad having a couple of drinks after work or my mom taking tranquilizers to deal with her stress."

* * * * * *

The "why" for getting high

Look It Up: Are those good reasons to do drugs? So we can feel good, escape, or cope with pressure? Not really. Consider:

• Moses' tough decision—"He chose to be mistreated along with the people of God rather than to enjoy the pleasures of sin for a short time" (Hebrews 11:25).

• King David's response to hard times—"Why are you downcast, O my soul? Why so disturbed within me? Put your hope in God, for I will yet praise him, my Savior and my God" (Psalm 42:5-6).

• Jesus' way to handle stress—(Mark 1:32-35).

Think It Through: Ken's statement that drugs are a form of amusement is interesting. The word amusement literally means "without thinking." In other words, "shut down your brain."

While God is not against us enjoying life, He is against the notion that we turn off our minds (2 Corinthians 10:5). He also is against the practice of pursuing pleasure through sin.

Work It Out: Instead of substance abuse, list some other ways people seek amusement or attempt to cope with the pressures of life.

Jot down how you would react to the pressure if:
1. Your best friend died.
2. Your boyfriend/girlfriend dropped you.
3. You were paralyzed in an accident.
4. Your parents put the heat on you to get a college scholarship.
5. You discovered you had cancer.

Nail It Down: See the factors that helped Moses choose long-term obedience rather than a lifestyle of temporary pleasure—Hebrews 11:26-27.

Pray About It:

TWO

35

For two night-marish years at Devlin High, Sheila was heavily involved with cocaine.

She's now drug-free. It wasn't easy—three months of isolation in a rehabilitation hospital followed by lots of counseling—but Sheila has come face to face with one of life's greatest mysteries.

"With not much else to do in the hospital, I started reading the Bible my mom sent me. And it hit me—like never before—that drugs are a big lie. They can't bring you happiness or take away your pain. Only Jesus can do that."

The big lie of a chemical high

Look It Up: Did you catch what Sheila just said? If not, hear the same truth again from the lips of Jesus Christ:

"'If anyone would come after me, he must deny himself and take up his cross and follow me. For whoever wants to save his life will lose it, but whoever loses his life for me and for the gospel will save it. What good is it for a man to gain the whole world, yet forfeit his soul? Or what can a man give in exchange for his soul?'" (Mark 8:34-37).

What a profound truth! What a strange paradox! We can never find real satisfaction or long-term happiness in drugs (or any other selfish pursuit). True fulfillment is found only in Christ.

Think It Through: The "Just Say No!" campaign is only a partial answer to the drug problem. People who say no to drugs—if they don't know Christ—still have emotional needs. Granted, they may not turn to drugs, but they will continue to look for something to fill the holes in their souls.

A more complete answer to the drug problem? "Just Say No! (to drugs)—Just Say Yes! (to Christ)."

Work It Out: Take a few minutes to quickly scan John's gospel. Carefully read every reference Jesus makes to life. How does His definition compare to what the world says life is all about?

Conclude your study with prayer. Ask God to help you grasp the fact that ultimate satisfaction is found only in Christ.

Nail It Down: Contemplate the words of Christ found in John 12:23-25.

******* THREE **DRUGS** ***********

If their skin, bones, and muscle tissue were transparent, the drug users at Devlin High just might change their ways.

Terry would be able to see the serious damage he's inflicted on his brain from his recreational use of Ecstasy.

Jennifer would freak at the sight of her diseased liver and kidneys. Too much glue sniffing, Jen.

Rob could enjoy a double thrill—by seeing how much harm marijuana smoking has done to his lungs, he might also get to watch his heart stop beating!

The high cost of a cheap thrill

Look It Up: The clearest Scriptural principle against drug use is this: "Do you not know that your body is a temple of the Holy Spirit, who is in you, whom you have received from God? You are not your own; you were bought at a price. Therefore honor God with your body" (1 Corinthians 6:19-20).

Get the message? God owns us. We're just tenants. We're supposed to honor Him by taking care of what is His property.

Since drugs damage the property, the issue is settled: We must avoid every kind of substance abuse.

Think It Through: Writer Chris Lutes states it well: "God calls our skin, with all of its stuffing, the temple of the Holy Spirit. Imagine the White House . . . Buckingham Palace. Yet for the Christian it's even better than all that. Because God lives in there. It's a holy place . . . So don't mess up the furnishings."

Work It Out: If drugs are a problem at your school, expose their dangers by:
• Writing an article for the school newspaper.
• Getting your teachers to invite medical doctors or drug counselors to discuss the problem.
• Starting an antidrug organization. (See below.)

Nail It Down: Read 2 Corinthians 6:16-18.

For help in starting an anti-drug organization at your school, contact:
• REACH (Responsible Adolescents Can Help), 14325 Oakwood Pl., N.E., Albuquerque, NM 87123; (505) 294-2929
• PRIDE (Parent Resource Institute for Drug Education), 50 Hurt Plaza, Suite 210, Atlanta, GA 30303; (404) 651-2548.

Pray About It:

****** **FOUR**

As he passes through a parking lot on the way to youth group, Richard, 16, looks with disgust at a group of "druggies" standing by a pickup truck. "What a bunch of losers!" he thinks.

One of the girls, 17-year-old Juanita, is hooked on crack. Her addiction is such that she'll do anything—beg on the street, steal, even prostitute herself—just to get enough cash for one more hit. To be truthful, Juanita is about as low as a person can go.

Jesus loves druggies!

Look It Up: From a human standpoint, does it seem that certain sins are especially bad, and that God, if He forgives them at all, does so only reluctantly?

No. The good news of Christ is that anyone can be forgiven. In fact, Jesus is the best friend a sinner could ever have.

"While Jesus was having dinner at Matthew's house, many tax collectors and 'sinners' came and ate with him and his disciples. When the Pharisees saw this, they asked his disciples, 'Why does your teacher eat with tax collectors and "sinners"?'

"On hearing this Jesus said, 'It is not the healthy who need a doctor, but the sick' " (Matthew 9:10-12).

Think It Through: How can you tell if someone you love is using drugs? Look for these symptoms:
- A decline in school or work performance
- Inexplicable mood changes
- Less concern with physical appearance
- Secretiveness when asked about social activities
- Disinterest in extracurricular activities or hobbies

Work It Out: If you think you might have a drug problem, remember first that you have a forgiving friend in Jesus. Second, talk to your youth leader or school counselor about getting some help.

If friends of yours are experimenting with drugs, pray for wisdom. Then gently communicate your concern, love, and desire to see them get help.

If someone you know is addicted to drugs, share that information with a mature Christian leader. Sometimes snitching on a friend is the best, most loving thing to do. It may even make the difference between life and death!

Nail It Down: On Saturday, consider the message of Luke 19:1-10. On Sunday, reflect on 1 Timothy 1:15.

✱✱✱✱✱✱✱ FIVE DRUGS ✱✱✱✱✱✱✱✱✱✱

DOUBT

When your faith takes a beating

Amazing how quickly things can change.

Yesterday you were standing strong, rock solid in your beliefs, feeling good about your faith. Today it's as though you've been ambushed spiritually. Suddenly, you're wondering about everything you've ever believed in!

Whether your current doubts stem from a perplexing personal experience, a disturbing discussion, or just a troubling question in your mind, the fact is that you need some answers.

Well, guess what? God's Word has the answers you're looking for!

"Stop doubting and believe" (John 20:27).

One night, as Caryn, Stacy, and Stephen (Stacy's older brother—a college sophomore) are staring up at the stars, Caryn muses aloud, "Isn't it amazing to think that God just spoke, and the heavens popped into existence?"

"What?" Stephen almost chokes. "Don't tell me you actually believe the Genesis creation account?"

"Of course I do! Why shouldn't I?"

Stephen spends the next 30 minutes attacking and ridiculing her literal belief in the Bible. At bedtime, Caryn is shaken.

The dilemma of doubt

Look It Up: Two Bible passages show two types of doubt.

1. The Jews. "Even after Jesus had done all these miraculous signs in their presence, they still would not believe in him" (John 12:37).

2. The father who asked Jesus if He could do anything to help his demon-possessed son. When Jesus answered, "'Everything is possible for him who believes,'" note the response:

"Immediately the boy's father exclaimed, 'I do believe; help me overcome my unbelief!'" (Mark 9:23-24).

In the first instance we see a stubborn unwillingness to believe in Jesus. It is brazen unbelief—in the face of overwhelming evidence. In the second case we see a wobbly faith, plagued by doubts. But, clearly, the man desires to believe more deeply.

Think It Through: The big difference between long-term unbelief and momentary doubt is this: One hardens us to the things of God. The other causes us to search for God more deeply.

Are you questioning your faith right now? If so, are you cynical—like the Jews in John 12—or skeptical—like the man in Mark 9?

Work It Out: Get together with a friend and write down all the things about your faith that you have questions about. Take the list to your Bible study leader and see if he or she can point you in the right direction. Then talk to God:

"Dear God, deepen my faith this week as I study Your Word. Use my doubts to draw me closer to You. Then show me how to overcome those doubts so that I can be more effective for You."

Nail It Down: Read about the results of long-term unbelief—John 3:18.

? ? ? ? ? ? ? ? ONE **DOUBT** ? ? ? ? ? ? ? ? ? ? ? ?

Derek has never felt comfortable around Skip, his youth leader. Skip oozes confidence and often gives the impression that "I don't have doubts about a thing. There are no questions in life that my faith can't handle."

Tonight, however, when Skip and Derek went out for a burger, Skip admitted, "My father's illness is starting to make me wonder about God's goodness."

That one simple admission made Derek feel closer to Skip and better about himself. Now he knows that even strong Christians struggle with doubt.

Even the wisest sometimes wonder

Look It Up: When John the Baptist first recognized Jesus as the Son of God, he turned to the gathered crowd and announced, "Look, the Lamb of God, who takes away the sin of the world!" (John 1:29). From that moment John's ministry (see John 1:30-36; Matthew 3) became a constant effort to point others to Christ.

And yet, notice what happened when John was arrested and dumped into Herod's dungeon. "When John heard in prison what Christ was doing, he sent his disciples to ask him, 'Are you the one who was to come, or should we expect someone else?'" (Matthew 11:2-3).

Think It Through: Jesus climbed all over John's case for doubting, right? No. As a matter of fact, Jesus had some very complimentary words to say about John (see Matthew 11:11-12).

Work It Out: The story of John's doubt is a both a good reminder and a good example for us.

1. The reminder? Even great men and women of God have doubts. (We're not spiritually immature just because we have questions. Take comfort in the fact that everybody has doubts at one time or another. You're not alone.)

2. The example? When John began questioning his beliefs, he turned to Christ, not away from Him. (Take your doubts to the Lord, ask for some real answers . . . and surround yourself with Christian friends!)

Nail It Down: Read about the doubt-plagued obedience of Abraham—Genesis 17:17-27.

? ? ? ? ? ? ? TWO

Pray About It:

41

You probably know someone like Kay.

A 15-year-old sophomore, she loves the Lord and wants, more than anything, to please Him. Though she trusted Christ when she was nine, and though she has seen Him do lots of things in and through her life, she is suddenly doubting her own salvation.

"What if I'm only kidding myself?" she keeps asking her mom. "What if I didn't believe hard enough?"

Such questions are starting to drive Mrs. Bennett crazy!

How God deals with doubters

Look It Up: Does God get impatient with those who are struggling with doubt? No!

"Now Thomas (called Didymus), one of the Twelve, was not with the disciples when Jesus came. So the other disciples told him, 'We have seen the Lord!'

"But he said to them, 'Unless I see the nail marks in his hands and put my finger where the nails were, and put my hand in his side, I will not believe it.'

"A week later his disciples were in the house again, and Thomas was with them. Though the doors were locked, Jesus came and stood among them and said, 'Peace be with you!' Then he said to Thomas, 'Put your finger here; see my hands. Reach out your hand and put it into my side. Stop doubting and believe.'

"Thomas said to him, 'My Lord and my God!' " (John 20:24-28).

Think It Through: How did Jesus respond to Thomas? By raking him over the coals? By getting impatient? No, he was very gentle. Nothing in the story indicates that Thomas was being hardhearted or cynical. Jesus realized that Thomas had honest doubts and that he really wanted to believe. And sure enough, he did!

Work It Out: Thomas's doubt was eased by examining the *wounds* of Jesus. Those who doubt their salvation can find peace by examining the *words* of Jesus.

Look up these verses and consider their meaning:
- John 1:12
- John 3:16
- John 5:24
- John 10:27-29
- John 11:25-26

The point? Jesus Christ has promised eternal life to those who trust in Him alone for salvation. Would Jesus lie?

Nail It Down: Read the promise of John 14:6-7.

? ? ? ? ? ? ? THREE **DOUBT** ? ? ? ? ? ? ? ? ? ? ? ?

If you think you have trials in your life, consider Stephanie's situation:

• She just found out she has scoliosis (abnormal curvature of the spine). She will have to wear a special brace—for a year!

• Her parents are transferring her to a different school—one that is tougher academically. (As if she wants to study harder than she already does!)

• The family dog may have to be put to sleep.

Stephanie's response? "Where is God in all this? Why doesn't He do something?"

Doubting your way to a deeper faith

Look It Up: When trials strike and cause us to doubt, James gives us this counsel:

"If any of you lacks wisdom, he should ask God, who gives generously to all without finding fault, and it will be given to him. But when he asks, he must believe and not doubt, because he who doubts is like a wave of the sea, blown and tossed by the wind. That man should not think he will receive anything from the Lord; he is a double-minded man, unstable in all he does" (James 1:5-8).

Think It Through: As you can see, doubt often results in uncertainty and insecurity. Yet, doubt can also be a positive force in our lives. Here's how: Doubt raises questions. Sincere questioning leads to searching. Honest searching leads to God. God provides answers. And answers, when accepted, result in a more stable faith.

As long as you don't wallow in your doubts and don't confuse doubt and defiance, you can actually make doubt work for you!

Work It Out: Facing trials? Restlessly doubting God's presence or perfect plan?

1. Ask for wisdom (James 1:5).
2. Believe that God's ways are best (James 1:6 . . . You may not feel this is true, but by faith, you must regard it as true.)
3. Expect God to replace your doubt with the wisdom of a stronger faith (James 1:17).

Pray this: "Father, I need wisdom. I don't understand what is happening, but You do. By faith (not feelings), I am trusting You right now. I believe Your ways are best. Amen."

Nail It Down: See Job's declaration of faith amidst trying circumstances—Job 23:10.

Pray About It: ⸻

? ? ? ? ? ? ? FOUR

Stephanie (the girl from yesterday's story) goes to her older sister for some advice.

"I don't know what to do, Amy," she says, addressing her sister through the door. "I feel so confused . . . I mean, I know in my head that there's a God and everything, but if I'm really honest, lately I don't know if I believe it in my heart."

Silence for about 30 seconds. When Amy emerges from the bathroom, she has a look of shock—or is it disgust?—on her face. "How can you say that? What are you? A stupid atheist or what?"

Caring for the confused

Look It Up: Scripture gives us several keys for dealing with those who doubt:
- Show mercy. "Be merciful to those who doubt" (Jude 22).
- Demonstrate acceptance. "Accept him whose faith is weak, without passing judgment on disputable matters" (Romans 14:1).
- Offer your help in a spirit of patience. "And we urge you, brothers . . . help the weak, be patient with everyone" (1 Thessalonians 5:14).

Think It Through: What would happen if you shared your deepest doubts with your parents? Your youth leader? Your best friend? Do you have anyone with whom you can share your doubts?

How would you feel if you were Stephanie? What would have been a more biblical way for Amy to respond?

Work It Out: When Christian family members or friends are questioning their faith, don't make life even more difficult for them.
1. Listen. (This is the most merciful thing you can do. By letting them verbalize their thoughts and feelings, you are helping them sort through their doubts.)
2. Avoid the temptation to judge. (Remember, feelings aren't right or wrong; they just are.)
3. Help. (Pray daily with and for your hurting friends. Direct them to wise counsel. Share Bible verses, books, and/or tapes that have helped you— but only after you have listened first!)

Nail It Down: On Saturday, reflect on Peter's experience with doubt—Matthew 14:22-33. On Sunday, consider the truth that involvement in activities you have doubts about is wrong—Romans 14:22-23.

??????? FIVE **DOUBT** ?????????????

SATAN

You can call him Mephistopheles, Beelzebub, Lucifer, or the Devil. But, no matter what you call him, Satan is alive and well. Satan worship, witchcraft, and occult practices are on the increase in the U.S. In fact, there are even Satanic "churches" throughout the U.S. dedicated to the worship of Satan!

Who is Satan? The first thing that comes to mind when someone mentions the Devil is a reddish being with long horns, a pointed tail, and a big pitchfork. For others who don't actually believe in his existence, "Satan" is simply a way to refer to the idea or presence of evil in the world. Yet, the Bible reveals that Satan is a real, personal, powerful creature who is active in our world (Luke 4:1-13).

Where did Satan come from? The Devil was at one time the most beautiful angel in heaven. Known as Lucifer, he was second only to God Himself (Ezekiel 28:12-15). But, because of the desire to be like God, Lucifer rebelled against God and was expelled from heaven along with one-third of all the angels (Revelation 12:4). Thus, Satan and his fellow demons are actually fallen angels.

What does Satan do? The Bible calls Satan "the god of this age" who blinds the minds of unbelievers to keep them from understanding and responding to the truth about Jesus Christ (2 Corinthians 4:4).

Satan is a powerful enemy of believers (Ephesians 6:11-18). We must take him seriously, remembering that a very real spiritual war is being fought all around us. Yet, as Christians we do not need to fear Satan. He was defeated by Christ at the Cross (Colossians 2:15). And even though he is now on the loose, the Devil's future defeat and final doom are certain (Matthew 25:41; Revelation 20:10).

Your response? Satan is real and he is powerful. Unfortunately, most believers usually go to one of two extremes: Either they disregard his role in the world, or they blame him for everything from nightmares to headaches. As a Christian you need to recognize Satan as your enemy. You must stand strong against him and not cower or panic, *"because the one who is in you is greater than the one who is in the world"* (1 John 4:4).

OMNI-WHAT?

Right now, you know where you are and what you're doing. But do you know where comedian Bill Cosby is and what's going on in his head? God does. Do you know exactly what you'll be doing Tuesday at 2:13 p.m.? God knows. Remember that object you misplaced a few weeks ago and still can't find? God sees it.

Theologians have a big word for this mind-boggling ability of God. They call it omniscience (pronounced om-nish-untz). *Omni* means all. *Scientia* means knowledge. Put them together and you've got the fact that God has total awareness, complete insight, infinite understanding, and universal comprehension. In simple terms, God knows everything.

Consider these Bible verses:

"O LORD, you have searched me and you know me. You know when I sit and when I rise; you perceive my thoughts from afar. You discern my going out and my lying down; you are familiar with all my ways. Before a word is on my tongue you know it completely, O LORD" (Psalm 139:1-3).

"Oh no! You mean God knows *everything* I do, say, and even think?"

Yes.

"Then He must *hate* me!"

No. It's just the opposite. God loves you intensely. And when you couple that love and concern with His total knowledge (not just of *actual* events, but also of all *possible* options), it follows that He alone can show you the best choices to make in life. As Jesus explained it:

"Are not two sparrows sold for a penny? Yet not one of them will fall to the ground apart from the will of your Father. And even the very hairs of your head are all numbered. So don't be afraid; you are worth more than many sparrows" (Matthew 10:29-31).

All this means far more than that God is merely a combination mind reader/bird watcher/hair counter. Because He has all knowledge, He is never caught off guard. Nothing takes Him by surprise.

Why wouldn't you trust a God who knows all about you and loves you anyway?

DEPRESSION
Those "bum me out" blues

Count all the people in this country who are in the 15-50 age group. Divide that number in half. The result is the number of people (according to expert projections) who will battle depression at some point in their lives.

Fifty percent! That explains why some baffled health professionals are using the term "epidemic." That also explains why we're spending a week to see what God says about this issue.

"The LORD is close to the brokenhearted and saves those who are crushed in spirit" (Psalm 34:18).

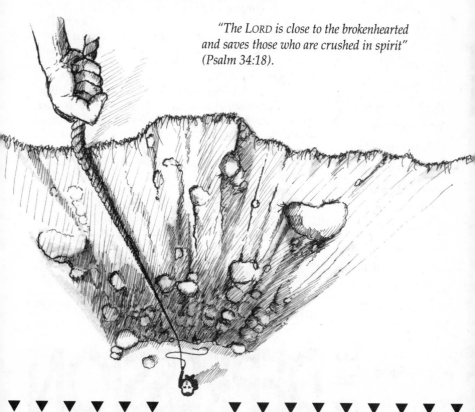

It's a cold, wet miserable day, and the cafeteria is like a morgue. People aren't talking much; they aren't smiling at all. A fellow student committed suicide over the weekend.

Rebecca and Tina are at a table by themselves whispering in low tones.

"I feel so depressed."

"You mean about Reggie?"

"Well, yeah. But I've been feeling blah for months now—long before this weekend. I try and try, but I can't seem to snap out of it, Tina. And that makes me feel even worse—Christians should never get down like this."

Depression is so . . . depressing!

Look It Up: The idea that a committed Christian can't get depressed is downright wrong! The Bible is full of examples of godly, depressed individuals:
- Moses (Numbers 11:10-15)
- Job (Job 6)
- King David—"How long, O LORD? Will you forget me forever? How long will you hide your face from me? How long must I wrestle with my thoughts and every day have sorrow in my heart?" (Psalm 13:1-2).
- The prophet Jeremiah— "Why did I ever come out of the womb to see trouble and sorrow and to end my days in shame?" (Jeremiah 20:18).

Think It Through: Other famous individuals have also battled depression—painter Vincent Van Gogh, President Abraham Lincoln, and British statesman Winston Churchill. Even Charles Spurgeon, one of the greatest preachers of all time, got down in the dumps. In fact, he was often confined to his bed for weeks at a time.

The point? If you suffer from the blues, or even from a more serious form of depression, you are not alone. Others have felt as you feel . . . and have found their way back to joy.

Work It Out: You fit in one of these two categories right now:
1. You feel depressed.
2. You know someone who feels depressed.

Either way, here's what to do. Declare war on the blues this week. Determine to learn all you can about the crippling emotional disorder called depression. And remember: There are no quick fixes, but in Christ there is real hope and healing!

Nail It Down: Can you relate to the feelings expressed in Psalm 77:1-9?

▼ ▼ ▼ ▼ ▼ ONE **DEPRESSION** ▼

A month later, Rebecca is more depressed than ever. She has gained 10 more pounds and is sleeping about 12 hours a day.

Tina is worried about her friend. She calls and invites her to do things with the group, but the response is always the same: "Thanks, but I'm just not in the mood. I just want to be by myself today."

When she isn't sleeping, Rebecca lies in bed, listening to really dark music.

"I wonder what happened to get her so bummed out?" Tina asks Margaret.

Why am I so down in the dumps?

Look It Up: According to God's Word, people may become depressed when they:
- Have an unthankful spirit (Numbers 14:1-4).
- Hold in their anger. "'In your anger do not sin': Do not let the sun go down while you are still angry" (Ephesians 4:26).
- Refuse to deal with sin. "When I kept silent [about my sins], my bones wasted away through my groaning all day long. For day and night your hand was heavy upon me; my strength was sapped as in the heat of summer" (Psalm 32:3-4).
- Suffer personal loss (Job 1-3).
- Try to live for God in their own strength (Romans 7).

Think It Through: A growing number of Christian counselors and doctors believe that depression may sometimes be caused by chemical imbalances or genetic deficiencies. Meanwhile, other leaders cite the anger caused by the breakdown of the family or early childhood traumas as the primary culprit.

Perhaps the blues may even be the result of various combinations of these factors.

By the way, do you see any of these factors at work in your life?

Work It Out: First, do a quick study of depression in an encyclopedia. Then ask your pastor, youth leader, or Sunday school teacher his or her views on the subject.

Second, pray: "Lord, You alone understand the roots of depression. Please protect me from its devastating effects. Help me to learn from the trying times without sinking into despair. Amen."

Nail It Down: How might turning to Christ eliminate depression for a non-Christian? See Ephesians 2:1-10.

Pray About It:

▼ ▼ ▼ ▼ ▼ T W O

For a long time Rebecca's depression wasn't getting any better. In fact, she began to lose hope that things would ever change. She could not stop her downward spiral. On three occasions, she seriously contemplated suicide.

Last night, however, while flipping through the channels on cable, Rebecca came across a call-in show that featured two Christian counselors who seemed really caring and wise.

Rebecca got excited and called. "Maybe this is what I need."

Things depressing disguise a blessing

Look It Up: Paul considered emotional weakness to be a blessing in disguise.

"But he [the Lord] said to me, 'My grace is sufficient for you, for my power is made perfect in weakness.' Therefore I will boast all the more gladly about my weaknesses, so that Christ's power may rest on me. That is why, for Christ's sake, I delight in weaknesses, in insults, in hardships, in persecutions, in difficulties. For when I am weak, then I am strong" (2 Corinthians 12:9-10).

Though he doesn't mention depression by name, his point is clear: Hard times are good if they cause you to turn to God and depend on His strength.

Think It Through: Do you know that it's okay to cry? In fact, it may be good for you! Some researchers believe that crying helps correct the chemical imbalances found in many depressed individuals. A good cry also releases stress that might otherwise lead to ulcers.

When was the last time you cried?

When was the last time you thanked God for a depressing situation?

Work It Out: If, for you, life is currently depressing, start looking for a blessing!

1. Use your experience to examine your own life.
2. Let your pain drive you close to God.
3. Take the lessons you learn and use them to build friendships with others who are hurting. (Record your feelings in a journal, so that when your depression is behind you, you will be able to remember just how low you felt.)
4. Draw strength from the promise in Isaiah 43:2.

Nail It Down: Want to read an amazing passage? Check out 2 Corinthians 1:8-11.

▼ ▼ ▼ ▼ ▼ THREE **DEPRESSION** ▼

Mona is emotionally flat. Not excited, not suicidal . . . just blah and gloomy. The exact reason for her down cycle isn't clear. Is it because she's gained five pounds? Did it start when she failed to receive even one Valentine last month? She's not sure.

After school today, at the suggestion of a friend, Mona went to the mall and purchased a new pair of faded blue jeans. She thought, "Maybe these will make me feel better."

Guess what? The jeans didn't do the trick.

Faded jeans can't fade your blues!

Look It Up: The Bible has a better prescription for beating the blues. Consider the case of Elijah the prophet.

After a time of great spiritual victory, he slipped into despair, "'I have had enough, LORD. . . Take my life.' . . . Then he lay down under the tree and fell asleep" (1 Kings 19:4-5).

That's when God went to work. He first brought him rest and refreshment (vv. 5-9). He then reassigned Elijah to service and reminded him of the other faithful servants of God (vv. 9-18).

Think It Through: Are you experiencing hopelessness? Lack of motivation? Difficulty communicating? A desire to sleep excessively or trouble sleeping? Low self-esteem? Behavior problems? Trouble concentrating?

If so, you may be suffering from a mild case of the blues. If you have these symptoms to an extreme degree, consult a trained professional—your family doctor, your guidance counselor, or your pastor. Real recovery can begin with a simple phone call!

Work It Out: Want to get out of the pits?

1. Ask for help. Ask God to do in your life what He did in Elijah's.

2. Tell a friend. Others cannot read your mind and are not always aware of your feelings.

3. Help someone else. Directing your focus outside yourself does wonders inside you.

4. Move around. You'd be amazed at how a physical fitness routine can improve your mood.

5. Be thankful. It's hard to be down when you're counting your blessings.

Nail It Down: Praise your way to a more joyful attitude—see Psalm 103.

Pray About It:

▼ ▼ ▼ ▼ ▼ FOUR

After struggling with depression for nearly three months, Rebecca (days 1–3) is finally recapturing a sense of joy in life. She has a bounce in her step. Her room-brightening smile is back too.

How did she recover?

Well, as we stated on day 1, there are no quick fixes, no easy answers. The healing came from a variety of factors. But surely one of the biggest reasons was Tina's patient love for her bummed out friend.

Inflating the depressed

Look It Up: Repeatedly the Bible requires that Christians sympathize with those who hurt:

• "Rejoice with those who rejoice; mourn with those who mourn" (Romans 12:15).

• "Carry each other's burdens, and in this way you will fulfill the law of Christ" (Galatians 6:2).

• "Therefore, as God's chosen people, holy and dearly loved, clothe yourselves with compassion, kindness, humility, gentleness and patience" (Colossians 3:12).

Tina put those verses into practice. We need to do the same with the Rebeccas in our lives.

Think It Through: Depressed individuals need your support, love, patience, and encouragement. They do not need you to blame them, lecture them, or argue with them about their condition.

Is there someone in your life who is down in the dumps? What can you do to help pull that individual out of the pits?

Work It Out: Pick one of these practical things and reach out in love to someone who's depressed:
1. Send a card.
2. Call and express your love and concern.
3. Visit the person and listen to him or her.
4. Give a hug.
5. Share a favorite joke.
6. Pray for your friend.
7. Go jogging together.
8. Bring that person to youth group and church.

Nail It Down: Read Acts 20:35. On Saturday, see the Lord's compassion for those who are hurting— Psalm 103:13. On Sunday contemplate the prophet Jeremiah's depression in Jeremiah 20:7-18. Look for clues as to how he overcame his case of the blues.

▼ ▼ ▼ ▼ ▼ FIVE **DEPRESSION** ▼

REPUTATION
How do others see you?

"I urge you to live a life worthy of the calling you have received" (Ephesians 4:1).

It's interesting to see the various reputations people gain. For instance: Sprinter Ben Johnson is considered a cheater. Preacher Billy Graham is regarded as a godly man. Actor Michael J. Fox is thought to be funny and cute. Tycoon Donald Trump is often viewed as conceited.

But it is not just the rich and famous who have reputations. Ever stop to think about how your friends and neighbors see you?

Sarah is walking down a hall at school. As she threads her way through the clusters of students, the people who look her way automatically review her reputation. They do it without thinking.

Here are some of the thoughts that pop into their heads when they consider Sarah: "sweet; nice—but a little too serious about God; Christian; smart."

From the other direction comes Bart. People take one glance at him and instantly think to themselves: "jerk; cocky; wild; handsome; arrogant; unpredictable; headed for trouble."

Worth more than silver or gold

Look It Up: Have you ever watched a wildlife show on TV and seen those sucker fishes (properly called remoras) that attach themselves to sharks and whales? Your reputation is like a remora. It goes with you everywhere. No wonder the Bible warns us to seek a good reputation by having a good name.
- "A good name is more desirable than great riches; to be esteemed is better than silver or gold" (Proverbs 22:1).
- "A good name is better than fine perfume" (Ecclesiastes 7:1).

Think It Through: When people hear your name, what words or images do you think come to mind?
If you died today, how would your tombstone read? Are you pleased with that reputation?

Work It Out: Rate your own reputation using the following scale (one represents "What a joke!"; five represents "an accurate description."

	1	2	3	4	5
• Hard working					
• Honest					
• Dependable					
• Godly					
• Joyful					
• Compassionate					
• Unselfish					
• Wise					
• Faithful					

Based on what you see in that chart, in which area(s) could you use a reputation overhaul?

Nail It Down: See how a "good name" was the main criterion used to choose the first deacons in Acts 6:1-7.

✦✦✦✦✦✦✦ ONE **REPUTATION** ✦✦

Guarding your own good standing

What does Sarah (see Day 1) do—if anything—to maintain such a good reputation?

Well, she attends a weekly Bible study for youth at her church. Plus she's careful to spend time reading the Bible and praying on her own every morning. Most important, she not only reads what the Bible says—she also does it.

As her Dad has told her numerous times, "Sarah, you just keep yourself straight with the Lord, and everything else will fall into place."

Look It Up: Moses taught the Israelites this same principle as they prepared to go into the Promised Land.

"See, I have taught you decrees and laws as the LORD my God commanded me, so that you may follow them in the land you are entering to take possession of it. Observe them carefully, for this will show your wisdom and understanding to the nations, who will hear about all these decrees and say, 'Surely this great nation is a wise and understanding people' " (Deuteronomy 4:5-6).

The lesson simply stated? Obedience to the Lord usually results in a good reputation.

Think It Through: Sarah's motive for reading the Bible and going to youth group is not to make others think she's spiritual and neat. She does those things solely because she wants to please God. Her number one goal is to be right with Him. Her good reputation is just a by-product of doing those good things.

Do you work at keeping a good reputation or do you work at keeping yourself right with God? Is it possible to have a good reputation and not be right with God? Is it possible to have a bad reputation and be right with God?

Work It Out: Sit down with a good Christian friend today and discuss your reputations. Each of you can pick one thing to do (or quit doing) that will lead to a closer walk with God. Hold each other accountable for the rest of the month. Then see if your reputation has improved as a result of your improved walk. (Here's betting it will be better!)

Nail It Down: Read about the importance of a good reputation among unbelievers—Colossians 4:5.

Pray About It: _____

✦ ✦ ✦ ✦ ✦ ✦ T W O

F rank could probably do the cause of Christ a lot of good these days by not telling people he's a Christian.

See, he's hanging out with a group of students who aren't exactly angelic in their behavior. As a result, Frank has developed some new habits—drinking, smoking, watching X-rated videos, shoplifting —all while continuing to go to church and youth group.

How do you reflect God's image?

Look It Up: Throughout the Bible, different individuals were chastised for bringing shame on God's name.

• "And wherever they went among the nations they profaned my holy name, for it was said of them, 'These are the LORD's people, and yet they had to leave his land.' I [the Lord] had concern for my holy name, which the house of Israel profaned among the nations where they had gone" (Ezekiel 36:20-21).

• "As it is written: 'God's name is blasphemed among the Gentiles because of you'" (Romans 2:24).

• "They claim to know God, but by their actions they deny him. They are detestable, disobedient and unfit for doing anything good" (Titus 1:16).

Think It Through: It's bad enough to have a rotten reputation. It's even worse to do rotten things and—at the same time—claim to be a Christian.

How do you feel when you see someone who professes to be a believer in Christ doing outrageous or even sinful things? How do you think God feels when individuals drag His name through the mud?

Is there anything about your life that is presently bringing shame on God's name?

Work It Out: Look up the word *hypocrite* in the dictionary. Does that word describe you right now? If so, apologize for tarnishing His name, and ask Him for the strength to be a better ambassador (2 Corinthians 5:20).

Remember: God isn't looking for perfect people, but He does expect us to live according to His standards. Why? Because the way we live affects others. Our behavior can make people hungry to know God . . . or it can leave a bad taste in their mouths!

Nail It Down: Notice how concerned Moses was about God's reputation—Numbers 14:13-16.

✦ ✦ ✦ ✦ ✦ ✦ **THREE REPUTATION** ✦ ✦

During middle school, Betty had sex with four different guys. Not surprisingly, she quickly developed a reputation for being "loose." Classmates began pronouncing her name "Beddy."

When she got to high school, Betty gave her life to Jesus Christ. No kidding, she really is like a new person. But now the "loose" reputation won't die. Even though Betty is no longer sexually active (and doesn't even want to be), the rumors and whispering persist.

"How can I show people that I've changed?" Betty groans.

Repairing a rotten reputation

Look It Up: After a history of "breathing out murderous threats against the Lord's disciples" (Acts 9:1), Saul did not exactly have a great reputation among Christians. Even after his conversion on the road to Damascus, he had a hard time convincing the members of the first-century church that he had truly changed. In fact, "When he came to Jerusalem, he tried to join the disciples, but they were all afraid of him, not believing that he really was a disciple" (Acts 9:26).

However, because Barnabas, an older, more mature Christian, stood up for him (v. 27), and because Saul continued to exhibit a changed lifestyle (vv. 28-30), he was able to repair his rotten reputation. Over time Saul, the Christian-hater, became know as Paul, an apostle of Jesus Christ.

Think It Through: Warning: A religious reputation will not get you into heaven. The Apostle Paul had a lot of religious credentials, but it was not until he trusted Christ that he found eternal life (Philippians 3:4-11).

Work It Out: Are you trying to revamp your reputation? Remember the lessons from Saul's life:
• Trust Christ—Changing your outer image is a waste unless you also have a changed inner identity (2 Corinthians 5:17).
• Find a "Barnabas" who will believe in you and disciple you.
• Be consistent. It takes many months (maybe even years) to undo a bad rep. Don't give up (Galatians 6:9).

Nail It Down: Consider how Mary Magdalene was able to change her reputation. Read Luke 8:2; Mark 15:40-41; John 19:25; Matthew 27:61; 28:1; and John 20:11-18.

Pray About It:

❖ ❖ ❖ ❖ ❖

FOUR

A week ago, a friend confided to Anita, "I think I'm pregnant. Will you go with me to have a test done?" Eager to show compassion, Anita agreed.

The next day the girls drove to a crisis pregnancy center. While they were waiting, Anita ran out to the car to get her purse.

As Anita was hurrying back inside, some classmates drove by and saw her. Now the whole school is hearing rumors that Anita is pregnant! Poor Anita can't tell the whole truth—she'd be ratting on her friend.

"My reputation is ruined! What can I do?"

Picking up the pieces

Look It Up: Consider a similar situation from the New Testatment:

"This is how the birth of Jesus Christ came about: His mother Mary was pledged to be married to Joseph, but before they came together, she was found to be with child through the Holy Spirit. Because Joseph her husband was a righteous man and did not want to expose her to public disgrace, he had in mind to divorce her quietly" (Matthew 1:18-19).

They weren't married yet . . . but Mary was pregnant! Imagine the whispers, the stares, the juicy gossip.

But Mary didn't groan and complain. Knowing that she was innocent of any wrong, she willingly accepted her situation as being a part of God's plan.

Think It Through: Be careful not to value your reputation more than you value God and His will.

In certain situations, do you worry more about looking good in front of others, or is your primary concern doing whatever pleases God?

Work It Out: Should you be concerned about your reputation? Yes! Is reputation the most important thing in the world? No!

Write this saying on a card and carry it with you today:

"I should be more concerned with my character than with my reputation. My character is what I really am. My reputation is just what others think I am."

Nail It Down: Read Luke 1:26-38. On Saturday, consider the reputation of the people mentioned in 3 John 3-6, and 12. On Sunday, reflect on the reputation enjoyed by Noah —Genesis 6:9.

✦✦✦✦✦✦✦ FIVE **REPUTATION** ✦

GOD
Curing mental meltdown

The most important concept humans must wrestle with is God: Who is He? What is He like? How can we know Him?

And yet the minute we finite creatures attempt to understand the infinite Creator, we find ourselves on the verge of mental meltdown. For, in actuality, what we are trying to do is comprehend the incomprehensible.

Fortunately, God has not left us to struggle in ignorance. He has revealed much about His nature in the pages of the Bible.

Would you like to see what He says about Himself?

"Grace and peace be yours in abundance through the knowledge of God and of Jesus our Lord" (2 Peter 1:2).

Glenda is reading quietly one day when she suddenly exclaims to her mom:

"Hey, look at this! I found a typographical error in the Bible. This verse spells the word *LORD* with all capital letters. But down here *Lord* is spelled with normal letters."

Yahweh—eternal, personal God

Look It Up: That's not a mistake, Glenda. The Bible uses different type styles to represent God's different names:

"Moses said to God, 'Suppose I go to the Israelites and say to them, "The God of your fathers has sent me to you," and they ask me, "What is his name?" Then what shall I tell them?'

"God said to Moses, 'I AM WHO I AM. This is what you are to say to the Israelites: "I AM has sent me to you." '

"God also said to Moses, 'Say to the Israelites, "The LORD, the God of your fathers—the God of Abraham, the God of Isaac and the God of Jacob—has sent me to you." This is my name forever, the name by which I am to be remembered from generation to generation. ' " (Exodus 3:13-15).

In calling Himself I AM (the Hebrew word is *Yahweh*) or the LORD, God was describing Himself as the eternal, unchanging God. *Yahweh* is the name most often used in the Old Testament to describe God's personal relationship with His people.

Think It Through: Consider these important points:

1. The names of God are not fancy labels which mankind created, but are the names by which God has revealed Himself, so we can know Him better.

2. The name *Yahweh* appears in most English Bibles as "LORD." The name *Adonai* is also translated "Lord," but it is printed with lower case letters.

Work It Out: Try this prayer for guidance:

"Dear God, the name *Yahweh* tells me that You are eternal and personal. Allow me to know You more fully as I study the primary names by which You have revealed Yourself in Scripture. Amen."

Nail It Down: Reflect on Exodus 34:5-7.

✝ ✝ ✝ ✝ ✝ ✝ ONE GOD ✝ ✝ ✝ ✝ ✝ ✝ ✝ ✝ ✝

Kirsten and Alex are walking out of the movie theater . . . and the film is only half over!

"Alex, why do they do that? Why can't anyone seem to make a movie without taking God's name in vain every two seconds? I can handle some things, but that really gets me."

"I know. They don't even know what they're saying! *God* is just a four letter word to them."

Kirsten smiles, "God only has three letters."

"Okay, smarty!"

"Elohim": a clue to the Trinity mystery

Look It Up: The first name for God used in the Bible is the Hebrew title *Elohim:* "In the beginning God [Elohim] created the heavens and the earth" (Genesis 1:1).

A few verses later the creation account adds these verses: "Then God [Elohim] said, 'Let us make man in our image, in our likeness . . .' So God [Elohim] created man in his own image" (Genesis 1:26-27).

Based on these (and more than 2,500 other usages), the name *Elohim* indicates the power and creative activity of God. The name may stem from either a Hebrew word meaning "the strong One," or from a similar root word meaning "fear."

So what's the point? Simply this: Such an awesome Creator deserves our respect, not our scorn!

Think It Through: The term *Elohim* is plural. Some scholars believe the plural form is an attempt to express in grammatical fashion the truth that God's greatness and majesty put Him in a class all by Himself. Others argue that the plural form implies that God is a Trinity.

Question: Which view is correct? *Answer:* Both viewpoints are credible. *Elohim* is used in passages that suggest God's singular essence. It is also used in passages that hint at the truth of the Trinity.

Work It Out: Hop on your bike and take a slow spin around the block. Observe with your eyes, your ears, your nose, your sense of touch. What makes more sense to you—that the world around you happened by accidental evolution or that it was specially created by our powerful Elohim?

Do you use the name God in a profane way? Determine, in His power, to stop today.

Nail It Down: Read Deuteronomy 6:4.

Pray About It:

✝ ✝ ✝ ✝ ✝   TWO

Adonai—our Lord and Master

Hey, Lawrence! What do you think about what you've been reading here the last two days?

"You mean all this stuff about Yahweh and Elohim?"

Yes.

"Well, I'm not sure it really applies to me. See, I already have a personal relationship with God. I believe that He created the world. And I don't take His name in vain."

That's great. But the question for today is this: Who is your Adonai?

"My what?"

Your Adonai, your Kurios?

"I have absolutely no idea what you're talking about."

Look It Up: *Adonai* is the Hebrew word for Lord. *Kurios* is Lord in the Greek of New Testament times. That title—*Lord*—is used of God hundreds of times in the Bible:

• "Moses said to the LORD, 'O Lord, I have never been eloquent' " (Exodus 4:10).

• "I will praise you, O Lord my God, with all my heart; I will glorify your name forever" (Psalm 86:12).

• "At that time Jesus said, 'I praise you, Father, Lord of heaven and earth, because you have hidden these things from the wise and learned, and revealed them to little children' " (Matthew 11:25).

Think It Through: The title *Lord* implies control or possession. It is often applied to humans by their servants (Numbers 12:11; 2 Samuel 10:3; 1 Kings 1:43). Used of God, the meaning is much more profound. As our sovereign Lord, God expects obedience from us. As our perfect Master, He also provides for our needs.

Work It Out: Examine the following spheres of your life. List who or what is Lord over your thoughts, words, and behavior in that area. In other words, list who or what determines how you function in each situation.
1. School
2. Dating life
3. Work
4. Relationships at home
5. Time with friends
6. Athletics
7. Religious activities

Discuss your findings with a Christian friend and pray together that you will surrender more of yourself to the Lord.

Nail It Down: See LORD, God, and Lord all used in the same verse—Deuteronomy 10:17!

THREE GOD

Brent is extremely nervous about pitching in an important baseball game tomorrow afternoon.

Gretchen feels sure that she is supposed to go on the youth retreat next weekend, but she doesn't have the $35 registration fee. The deadline is tonight.

Thomas dreads visiting his dad tonight. "He always makes fun of my faith. I never know what to say."

Some other divine aliases

Look It Up: Those anxious, hurting individuals could find real encouragement by studying some of the other names by which God has revealed Himself in the Bible.

1. Variations of *Elohim:*
• *El Shaddai* ("God Almighty")—"When Abram was ninety-nine years old, the LORD appeared to him and said, 'I am God Almighty'" (Genesis 17:1). Other instances of this name (Genesis 28:3-4; Psalm 91:1-2) indicate that it implies, not only power, but provision and protection as well.
• *El Elyon* ("God Most High"—Genesis 14:19)
• *El Olam* ("Eternal God"—Genesis 21:33)

2. Variations of *Yahweh* (or *Jehovah*):
• *Yahweh-jireh* ("The LORD will provide")—"So Abraham called that place The LORD Will Provide" (Genesis 22:14).
• *Yahweh-rapha* ("The LORD who heals"—Exodus 15:26)
• *Yahweh-nissi* ("The LORD is my Banner," that is, the One who fights my battles—Exodus 17:8-15).
• *Yahweh-shalom* ("The LORD is Peace"—Judges 6:23-24)

Think It Through: Which aspect of God just revealed means the most to you? Which aspect of God's character does your best friend need to hear about?

Work It Out: What is it that you need most right now? Peace? Strength? Healing? Help? Call God by His appropriate name and trust Him to meet that need.

Pick out one of the verses just cited, copy it, and carry it with you today.

Nail It Down: Read about another name for God (*El Roi*—the God who sees our trouble and pain)—Genesis 16:13.

Pray About It: ──────────────────

 † † † † † **FOUR**

David is like a lot of people. He tends to think that God is just a heavenly version of his earthly dad. Consequently, David imagines God to be an excellent provider, who is distant, stern, demanding, and impatient—not someone you can be really close to.

Meanwhile, Serina also bases her concept of God on her father, so she lives with the constant fear that something awful is about to happen to her.

Infinite God, infinite list of names!

Look It Up: As we saw yesterday, a study of the names of God can do wonders for our bad attitudes and scared feelings. And if you think we've uncovered all the Biblical names for God, well, think again! He is also called:
- King (Psalm 47:7)
- Rock (This means that God is strong and unchanging. See Deuteronomy 32:3-4.)
- Fortress—"Turn your ear to me, come quickly to my rescue; be my rock of refuge, a strong fortress to save me" (Psalm 31:2).
- Husband (This refers to His faithful love for His people. See Isaiah 54:5 and Jeremiah 3:14)
- Shepherd (Psalm 23:1)
- Father—"If you, then, though you are evil, know how to give good gifts to your children, how much more will your Father in heaven give good gifts to those who ask him!" (Matthew 7:11).

Think It Through: Think of the best earthly dad you know. Our heavenly Father is infinitely better than that! He loves us and wants only the very best for us.

What about the current trend to try to eliminate all the male references to God in Scripture? If the Bible is inspired by God, is it right to do this?

Work It Out: For the rest of the month, keep a "God" journal. Write down every reference to God you come across in your Bible reading. Jot down your thoughts and feelings. Record prayers to God . . . and His answers to prayer. Include any other good quotes or insights you come across. (Warning: You may find keeping a journal so rewarding that you can't stop at the end of the month!)

Nail It Down: Think about Psalm 18:2. On Saturday, reflect on Proverbs 18:10. On Sunday, consider the intriguing name of God found in Exodus 34:14.

✝ ✝ ✝ ✝ ✝ ✝ FIVE **GOD** ✝ ✝ ✝ ✝ ✝ ✝ ✝ ✝ ✝ ✝

SEVEN REASONS
TO READ AND STUDY YOUR BIBLE

pro·pi'ti·a'tion, *n.*
1. Act of propitiating. 2.
Theol. That which propitiates.

Ooooo...
HE'S DREAMY!

S even (Not Necessarily Logical) Reasons to Read and Study Your Bible:

1. You'll be able to answer all the Bible questions on TV game shows.

2. Serious Bible study can burn more than 100 calories per hour.

3. A man in California once found a $100 bill in the pages of his Old Testament.

4. You'll be able to amaze your friends by knowing cool words like "propitiation" and "justification."

5. When your parents say, "Don't forget to take out the garbage tonight," it sounds real holy to be able to say, "Okay, but right now I'm *studying the Bible*." (They might even raise your allowance!)

6. You'll be able to point out the inaccuracies in all those movies about Jesus that are on TV at Easter time.

7. Studying the Bible is much cheaper than buying a new car and much safer than driving one.

S even (Really Good) Reasons to Read and Study Your Bible:

1. The Bible is like a letter to you from the God of the universe. In it God reveals the truth about Himself and how we can *know* Him, not just know *about* Him.

2. The Bible tells you how you can know for sure if you have eternal life (1 John 5:11-13).

3. You'll see how God has been involved in history.

4. You'll discover God's will for your lifestyle—how He wants you to live and why His way is best.

5. You'll see just how special you are to God . . . and how much He loves you.

6. In a wishy-washy culture, you'll find the Bible to be an awesome absolute—a source of strength and a reliable anchor to keep you steady in life's storms.

7. You'll find comfort when the world's got you down.

UNUSUAL
BIBLE STORIES

Forty-two kids were mauled by a couple of bears after they teased the prophet Elisha for being bald (2 Kings 2:23-25).

• While some prophets were chopping down trees, one of their iron ax-heads flew off and plopped into the Jordan River. Elisha cut a stick, threw it in the river, and the axhead floated to the surface (2 Kings 6:1-7).

• Eglon, king of Moab, was so fat that when Ehud, Israel's deliverer, rammed his sword into the king's belly, even the sword's handle disappeared (Judges 3:20-22).

• King David's son Absalom rode his mule under an oak tree and got his head caught in some branches. The mule kept going, leaving Absalom "hanging," very much alive. When Joab heard of the incident, he went and used Absalom, his bitter enemy, for javelin practice (2 Samuel 18:9-15).

• During an extreme drought, God directed a flock of ravens to bring bread and meat to the prophet Elijah every morning and evening (1 Kings 17:1-6).

• While listening to the great Apostle Paul preach late one night, a young man named Eutychus fell asleep. Unfortunately, he was sitting in a third-story window. As you might imagine, the fall was lethal. Paul quit preaching, went downstairs, raised the man from the dead, and then went back upstairs and finished his sermon (Acts 20:7-12).

• Some Israelites were burying a man when they spotted a band of raiders. They dumped the body into the prophet Elisha's tomb (either so they could run or possibly to fight). *"When the body touched Elisha's bones, the man came to life and stood up on his feet"* (2 Kings 13:20, 21).

GUILT
Freedom from shame

E ver felt it? The sickening feeling in the pit of your stomach—the haunting heaviness that keeps asking, "Why did you do that? Why? Why? Why?"

Of course you have. Guilt is a universal fact of life. It is something from which we try to escape but with which we all end up wrestling.

The next five pages are dedicated to every teenager who has ever asked, "How can I deal with the guilt in my life?"

"My guilt has overwhelmed me like a burden too heavy to bear" (Psalm 38:4).

Jenny wakes up on Sunday morning feeling especially guilty. She and her boyfriend got way too physical last night. They didn't go all the way, but they went much farther than Jenny ever intended.

In the evening, Jenny calls a friend, and explains the situation. What advice does she get?

"Forget about it, Jen! You were a saint not to go all the way! If anyone is guilty, it's that super-strict church of yours for making you feel so bad!"

Guilt began in the garden

Look It Up: Though the world declares guilt to be an obsolete remnant of our "religious past," the Bible insists that people feel guilty because they are guilty!

• "Everyone has turned away, they have together become corrupt; there is no one who does good, not even one" (Psalm 53:3).

• "All of us have become like one who is unclean, and all our righteous acts are like filthy rags; we all shrivel up like a leaf, and like the wind our sins sweep us away" (Isaiah 64:6).

• "If we claim to be without sin, we deceive ourselves and the truth is not in us" (1 John 1:8).

Think It Through: Suppose a ruthless criminal guns down an elderly lady in cold blood . . . and then laughs. Is the man guilty? Of course! Does he feel guilty? No. In his own perverted way, he feels good—even glad—about what he did.

Guilt is more than a feeling. In fact, it is best defined as the condition of being in violation of moral and/or civil laws. Guilt may be accompanied by feelings of remorse or sorrow, but it doesn't have to be. A person can be guilty without feeling guilty.

Work It Out: Discuss these questions/statements with a close Christian friend.

1. What would make you feel more guilty than anything else?

2. What advice would you give to a guilty friend like Jenny?

3. The way to overcome guilt is to————.

4. I am guilty right now of ——————.

5. If I could erase one guilty memory from my past, it would be the time I ——————.

Nail It Down: See where guilt began. Read Genesis 3:1-10 (especially v. 10).

▶▶▶▶▶▶ **ONE GUILT** ▶▶▶▶▶▶▶▶▶

It's Tuesday and Jenny is still feeling bad over what happened on Saturday night (see yesterday's story).

The more she replays the scene in her head, the sadder she gets. "Why did I let that happen? I knew better. I'm such an idiot!"

Feeling too unworthy to pray, Jenny tries to escape her guilt by doing her homework. When that doesn't work, she picks up a novel she has been reading. She can't concentrate at all.

Finally, in desperation, she clicks on the TV.

The marks of a guilty person

Look It Up: How do people respond to guilt?
• Some don't even know they're guilty!—"They are darkened in their understanding and separated from the life of God because of the ignorance that is in them due to the hardening of their hearts" (Ephesians 4:18).
• Some feel bad (Matthew 26:74-75).
• Some try to escape (Jonah 1:1-6).
• Some get depressed (Psalm 40:12).
• Some get physically sick—"When I kept silent, my bones wasted away through my groaning all day long. For day and night your hand was heavy upon me; my strength was sapped as in the heat of summer" (Psalm 32:3-4).
• A few repent (Psalm 51:1-12).

Think It Through: According to at least one survey of mental health professionals, the major problem of almost half of the people in the institutions in this country is guilt. It's been said that many of these patients could be restored to health if they could just know that they were forgiven!

Do you think Jenny will be to deal with her guilt using the approach she has chosen?

Is guilt a regular part of your life right now? How, if at all, are you responding to it?

Work It Out: Try to list some additional methods that people use to try to avoid a sense of guilt.

Pray this: "Lord, please search my heart and show me where I am guilty of wrong actions, thoughts, or words. More than anything else, I want to be right with You. In Jesus' name, Amen."

Nail It Down: Extreme guilt—if not dealt with—can lead to suicide! See Matthew 27:3-5.

Pray About It:

TWO

▶▶▶▶▶▶

Try as she might, Jenny cannot stop thinking about her overly passionate date on Saturday night.

The guilt is like a giant weight. She feels a deep sadness in her heart and a sick feeling in her stomach. Unable to concentrate on anything, Jenny is unsettled and extremely restless.

In desperation, she finally pulls out her Bible and turns to Psalm 51. As she reads the words, she begins to cry.

Is guilt ever good?

Look It Up: Guilt can actually end up being a good thing. Often it is not until we are broken and helpless that we sense our need for God's forgiveness and restoration.

Do you remember the story of the prodigal son—the guy who left home, wasted his inheritance in a spree of wild living, and hit rock bottom? Do you remember what happened next?

"When he came to his senses, he said . . . 'I will set out and go back to my father and say to him: Father, I have sinned against heaven and against you.' . . . So he got up and went to his father" (Luke 15:17-20).

Let your guilt help to point you back to God.

Think It Through: Kudzu is a weed that grows like crazy and is practically impossible to exterminate. People chop it, burn it, and poison it, but killing it for good takes extreme measures.

Guilt is kind of like kudzu. You can, by your own efforts, get rid of it, but that takes a long time and a lot of effort. And in the process, you'll also damage your conscience (1 Timothy 4:2)!

Work It Out: Don't try to eliminate guilty feelings without facing up to the cause of those feelings. That's like treating the symptoms but ignoring the real disease! Instead, let your guilt propel you toward God.

Ask God to show you why you feel guilty. Because He is kind, He will do that. Then let that kindness lead you to repentance (Romans 2:4).

Hey, why wallow around in a pigpen of guilt (Luke 15:15-16), when you can enjoy the forgiveness and the blessing of God (Luke 15:20-24)?

Nail It Down: Read how King David responded to guilt—Psalm 32:5.

▶ ▶ ▶ ▶ ▶ ▶ THREE GUILT ▶ ▶ ▶ ▶ ▶ ▶ ▶ ▶ ▶

Because of her sin last Saturday night, notice what Jenny is doing. She is talking with God about her guilt; she is looking to Him for forgiveness.

Notice all the things Jenny is not doing to end her guilt—she isn't trying to pay for her own sins; she isn't seeking to earn forgiveness; she isn't attempting to explain away her failure; and she isn't blaming anyone else.

Afterwards, Jenny doesn't feel forgiven, but she believes that she is, based on the promises of God's Word.

The right way to get rid of guilt

Look It Up: If you're about to wilt because of guilt, Jenny's actions are worth another look:

1. Admit your sin (Hosea 5:15). You must be willing to face up to your guilt and take full responsibility for your actions and attitudes.

2. Believe that God is willing to forgive you. "If we confess our sins, he is faithful and just and will forgive us our sins and purify us from all unrighteousness" (1 John 1:9).

3. Renew your commitment to obey God. "Now make confession to the LORD, the God of your fathers, and do his will" (Ezra 10:11).

Think It Through: Let's repeat the important point we made yesterday: You cannot remove your own guilt. Lady Macbeth (of Shakespearean fame) couldn't. Pontius Pilate also tried (and failed) to wash his hands of the blood of Christ and clear his guilty conscience (Matthew 27:24-26).

Is it really possible that Jenny has found forgiveness, even though she doesn't feel forgiven?

Work It Out: If you have never trusted Jesus Christ to forgive your sins, you stand "guilty" before a holy God. Only by accepting Christ's sacrifice can you be declared "not guilty."

Or perhaps you already have trusted Christ as your Savior, but you haven't been living like a child of God. If that is the case, acknowledge your disobedience to God, claim the forgiveness you enjoy in Christ, and trust Him for the power to "live a new life" (Romans 6:4).

Nail It Down: Find a copy of The Living Bible and read Romans 3:21-31.

Pray About It:

▶ ▶ ▶ ▶ ▶ ▶ FOUR

71

Good news to report to you here on Day 5!

Jenny has taken steps to protect against another Saturday night disaster. She has talked at length with her boyfriend, and they have set some newer, higher standards for their relationship (more double dates, lots of group activities, no getting alone in the dark.)

Plus, Jenny has started a Scripture memory program. As she memorizes and meditates on Scripture, she is beginning to understand more and more about God's incredible forgiveness.

The fine freedom of forgiveness

Look It Up: Forgiveness is fantastic for a number of reasons.

1. It brings us peace with God. "Therefore, since we have been justified through faith, we have peace with God through our Lord Jesus Christ" (Romans 5:1).

2. It means God forgets our sinful acts. "Then he adds: 'Their sins and lawless acts I will remember no more' " (Hebrews 10:17).

3. It helps us overcome a guilt-ridden past (1 Timothy 1:12-17).

4. It brings a renewed sense of joy (Psalm 51:12; Romans 4:6-8).

Think It Through: Occasionally Christians wrestle with guilt even after confessing their sins. According to the Bible, they are forgiven (1 John 1:9), but they still don't grasp this fact. This is known as false guilt.

The source of these feelings is described in Revelation 12:10. There Satan is called "the accuser of our brothers, who accuses them before our God day and night." Are you suffering from false guilt?

Work It Out: The best way to avoid the guilt trap is to avoid sin in the first place! Here are some tips for doing just that—today and every day:
- Dedicate yourself to God (Romans 12:1).
- Put on God's armor (Ephesians 6:10-18).
- Immerse yourself in God's Word (Psalm 119:11).
- Associate with believers (Hebrews 10:24-25).
- Remind yourself frequently of the serious consequences of sin (Galatians 6:7).
- Walk in the power of the Holy Spirit (Galatians 5:16-26).

Nail It Down: Read Psalm 103:12. On Saturday, reflect on Micah 7:19. On Sunday, consider Isaiah 44:22.

▶▶▶▶▶▶▶ FIVE **GUILT** ▶ ▶ ▶ ▶ ▶ ▶ ▶ ▶ ▶

CONTENTMENT
The formula for happiness

Disease research is big news these days. New findings about AIDS, encouraging updates about cancer, reports from the American Heart Association—the fact is we hear *constantly* about life's most threatening illnesses.

All except one.

This particular infirmity invades the spirit—afflicting millions (perhaps even billions) of individuals with a devastating sense of dissatisfaction. *You* may even be infected.

But don't be alarmed. *This* disease has a cure. It's called contentment.

"But godliness with contentment is great gain" (1 Timothy 6:6).

It's 6:30 A.M. in Centerville. That means the grumbling is just beginning.

• Sixteen-year-old Simone takes a quick inventory of her closet. Thenshe slumps backward across the bed. "My clothes are the worst in the history of the world!" she sighs.

• As 15-year-old Wendell stubs his toe on his little brother's bed, he mutters, "&%$#@*, I want my own room!"

• Blake, 16, looks in the mirror with disgust. "That does it! I'm joining the health club today!"

Stumbling begins with grumbling

Look It Up: A quick way to find out if you've got the disease of dissatisfaction is to listen to what comes out of your mouth. If complaining and grumbling are part of your regular conversation, look out!

Despite deliverance from Egyptian bondage and miraculous provision from above, the Israelites constantly complained. They were never content! Over and over again they whined (Numbers 11; 14:2-4; 16:11, 41; 20:2-5; 21:4-7). Finally God said, "How long will this wicked community grumble against me? . . . They will meet their end in this desert; here they will die" (Numbers 14:27, 35).

Think It Through: Listen carefully: It is not wrong to have nice clothes, your own room, or a good physique. It's not even wrong—up to a point—to want these things. The problems begin when we forget all that we do have, and focus on what we don't have.

Have you been grumbling a lot lately? What are the areas in your life where you find the most dissatisfaction?

Work It Out: Start your week-long study of contentment by doing these five things:

1. Tell God you're sorry for the times you've complained last week.
2. Ask Him to help you change your focus this week.
3. Invite a friend to study the topic of contentment with you.
4. Memorize the verse on the previous page.
5. Look around your room and thank God for some of the things you do possess.

Nail It Down: Read 1 Corinthians 10:10-12 and Philippians 2:14.

♥ • • • • • ♥ ONE **CONTENTMENT** ♥

Let's see what's happening with Simone. (You'll recall that yesterday she was lamenting the sad state of her wardrobe.) As we catch up with her, she's in the mall—and her mood is deteriorating rapidly!

"All my friends have nice clothes, and I have to dress like some kind of street person. Then I come to the mall and I can't find anything decent for under $50!

"Why doesn't my family have more money? I just want a few nice outfits."

A bad case of the "I wants"

Look It Up: Some people, like Simone, want more clothes. For others the wish list includes a nicer car (or even just a car, period), a better stereo, or just some extra cash. Whatever the want, we all need to remember this fact:

"For we brought nothing into the world, and we can take nothing out of it" (1 Timothy 6:7).

We also need to adopt the apostle Paul's attitude:

"But if we have food and clothing, we will be content with that" (1 Timothy 6:8).

Think It Through: Question: How do manufacturers and merchants get us to buy their products or services? Answer: They spend billions of dollars each year on advertising. Each ad is carefully designed to make us feel discontented: "My car is a bomb; I need a new one" or "My clothes are the worst; time to go shopping" or "My body is a wreck; I'll join the health club."

Advertisers know that feeding our dissatisfaction works like a charm!

Work It Out: See if this helps:

1. Make a list of all the material things that you wish you had. Don't hold back—write everything down.

2. Pray this: "Father, as my list indicates, I have a bad case of the 'I wants.' Instead of seeking Your kingdom first (Matthew 6:33), I've been seeking things first. Change me, Lord. Help me to become less attracted to stuff and more devoted to You. Right now I lay all my desires on the altar of Your will. Do as you see fit. Amen."

3. Take the list and burn it.

Nail It Down: Read Hebrews 13:5.

Pray About It:

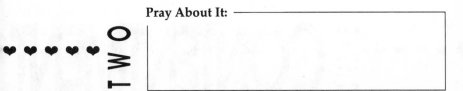

♥ ♥ ♥ ♥ ♥

T W O

L et's catch up with Wendell. When we last saw him (Day 1), he was pretty hot about his family's close living quarters. There he is now . . .

"Hey, Wendell, how's it going?"

"Man, back off! You're just like my family— always up in my face, cramping my style. I guess I won't be finding any peace until I can get out on my own!"

"Whoa, dude —sorry we asked!"

Joy in the midst of a bad situation

Look It Up: If, like Wendell, you're facing an unpleasant situation, listen to Paul's words:

"I have learned to be content whatever the circumstances. I know what it is to be in need, and I know what it is to have plenty. I have learned the secret of being content in any and every situation, whether well fed or hungry, whether living in plenty or in want" (Philippians 4:11-12). "Content whatever the circumstances . . . in any and every situation." Wow! What's the secret? This: "I can do everything through him who gives me strength" (v. 13).

Think It Through: How would you react in the following situations:

• You get so sick that you have to repeat the whole school year.
• Your dad gets transferred and you have to move away from all your friends.
• You go three months (or longer) without a date.
• You get cut from the team at school.
• Your family moves into a tiny apartment right next door to Wendell.

Work It Out: If you're in an unpleasant situation today, reach for the help available in Philippians 4:13.

Potential—We can "do everything"! (So smile, be thankful, find a silver lining, and turn what's bad into good.)

Person—We know "Him," the source of all true contentment. (Focusing on the awesomeness of our heavenly Father puts our problems in perspective.)

Power—We can count on His strength. (We must trade our frustrations and weaknesses for His might.)

Nail It Down: Discover contentment no matter what the circumstances—Philippians 4:19.

♥ ♥ ♥ ♥ ♥ THREE **CONTENTMENT**♥

Blake was last seen on Day 1, searching the mirror for signs of muscle and dejectedly vowing to take up body building.

Granted, Blake's no Schwarzenegger, but let's be objective—he's no poster child for world hunger either. At 5'10" and 160 pounds, he looks pretty decent. He's not overweight, he's well proportioned, and nobody has ever singled out his rear end as being oversized!

The truth is, there are a lot of guys who would gladly trade for Blake's physique.

Unhappy with the way you look?

Look It Up: There has never been a time in history when a culture has been as obsessed with physical fitness and appearance as ours is right now.

Liposuction is now the number-one type of cosmetic surgery. The number of gyms and spas is mushrooming. Home exercise equipment sales are exploding. What does all this mean? People are dissatisfied with the way they look, and they're willing to do almost anything to change their appearance.

Consequently, these words are appropriate for us:

"Train yourself to be godly. For physical training is of some value, but godliness has value for all things, holding promise for both the present life and the life to come" (1 Timothy 4:8)

Think It Through: It isn't wrong to be on an exercise program. But it is wrong to become obsessed with your appearance—to never be content with your looks.

Remember four things:
- God made you the way you are.
- Perfect looks are impossible to attain.
- Good looks are hard to keep.
- Outer appearance has only limited value.

Work It Out: Now, do these four things:

1. Evaluate how much emphasis you put on looks.

2. Evaluate on a scale of 1–10 how contented you are with your looks (1 means "gag me with a barbell"; 10 means "Thank you, Lord, for the way You have made me").

3. Ask God to give you His perspective on the importance of physical appearance.

4. Look at yourself in a mirror and point out the good features you do have.

Nail It Down: Consider the message of 1 Samuel 16:7.

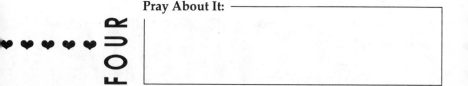

Pray About It:

❤ ❤ ❤ ❤ ❤ FOUR

Six months after the events of Day 1 and we find:

• Simone has a job at a clothing store that entitles her to a 25 percent employee discount. She's beefed up her wardrobe, yet she still isn't satisfied.

• Wendell, after reading and applying the lessons found on the previous four pages, is much more contented. He still wants his own room, but won't let cramped conditions steal his joy.

• Blake has packed on the muscle by pumping iron and popping steroids. His body looks great, but now his face is breaking out and his hair is falling out!

The quest for true satisfaction

Look It Up: We need to learn at least two things from the folks in Centerville:

1. By looking for lasting satisfaction in the things of this world, we find only disappointment (1 John 2:17).

2. By seeking to know and obey the Lord, we find true contentment. Then, and only then, can we say with the psalmist:

"Whom have I in heaven but you? And earth has nothing I desire besides you. My flesh and my heart may fail, but God is the strength of my heart and my portion forever" (Psalm 73:25-26).

Think It Through: Be objective for just a minute. Put aside all your "I wants" and your "I wish I hads."

As a Christian, you have a real relationship with the one true God. You have been blessed with every spiritual blessing in Christ (Ephesians 1:3). What's more, you live in one of the most prosperous nations on earth.

What is there to be dissatisfied about?

Work It Out: If you want to develop an attitude of contentment, it may be necessary for you—at least temporarily—to do one or more of the following: stay out of the stores, leave the TV off, quit looking at certain magazines, avoid hanging around greedy people, and spend extra time in God's Word.

Which of those action steps do you most need? Will you make that commitment today?

Nail It Down: On Saturday, read Proverbs 15:16-17. On Sunday, consider if you could truthfully pray Psalm 17:15.

❤ ❤ ❤ ❤ ❤ ❤ FIVE CONTENTMENT

STRANGE
BUT TRUE, BIBLE FACTS

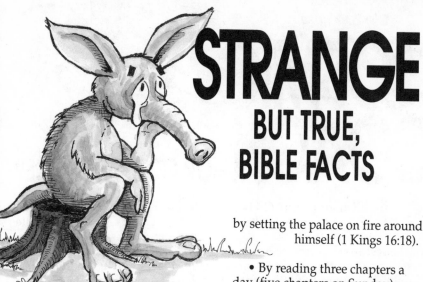

by setting the palace on fire around himself (1 Kings 16:18).

• By reading three chapters a day (five chapters on Sunday) you can read through the whole Bible in a year.

• Aardvarks are never mentioned in the Bible.

• The shortest prayer in the Bible is Peter's—"Lord save me!" (Matthew 14:30).

• At the age of 10, Abraham Lincoln had read the entire Bible three times.

• The longest name in the Bible is Maher-shalal-hash-baz (aren't you glad Isaiah wasn't *your* dad?) It means "Quick to the plunder, swift to the spoil" (see Isaiah 8:3).

• The names *Joshua* and *Jesus* mean the same thing: "Jehovah is salvation."

• Zimri was king of Israel for one week when he committed suicide

• When Joshua was leading the children of Israel in battle against the Amorites, God slowed down the rotation of the earth, resulting in constant daylight for almost 48 hours. This gave the Israelites time to conquer their enemies (Joshua 10:12-14).

• The word *Bible* comes from the Greek word *biblios* and means "book."

• In the King James Version of the Bible, Ezra 7:21 contains every letter of the alphabet except *j*.

• Matthew 18:10 indicates that children have personal angels.

• God is never mentioned in the Book of Esther.

COSMIC COACH
OR GOD OF GRACE?

Some Christians picture God as stern and demanding—sort of a cosmic football coach. Stalking the heavenly sidelines, He makes notes on a giant clipboard and constantly yells things like, "C'mon! Get it together down there!" and "Okay, you bunch of knuckle-heads—I've had just about enough of your clowning around!"

"Since God keeps all those checklists and stat sheets," some people reason, "I'd better perform *perfectly*. Otherwise God won't accept me. Any serious mistakes and He'll yank me out of the game!"

What a lie! God doesn't relate to us on the basis of what we do or don't do. That's living by the law. No, He relates to us on the basis of what *Christ* has done. That's living by grace.

That's why trusting in Jesus' death is so radical. It means we are accepted. Completely. Right now. The pressure's off. The freedom's on.

The following chart shows the difference between living by law and living by grace. Which column best describes your life with God?

The Bondage of Law (Galatians 3:23-25)	The Freedom of Grace (Romans 3:21-31)
drudgery ("All these *rules* are killing me!")	**joy** ("This *relationship* is great!")
fear ("God may zap me!")	**peace** ("Jesus took the full punishment for my sins!")
futility ("I'm struggling to *earn* His acceptance!")	**victory** ("I know I can't *earn* His acceptance . . . but I can *receive* it by faith!")
condemnation ("I'm dirty and gross!")	**justification** ("I am righteous in His sight!")
weakness/inability ("I can't!")	**power** (*"He* can!")
emphasis on my performance ("I *have* to be good!")	**emphasis on my position** ("Because of who I am in Christ, I *want* to be good!")

Aren't you glad our heavenly Father is a God of grace? Don't you think it's about time you started relating to Him on that basis?

✗ ✗ ✗ ✗ ✗ ANGER ✗ ✗ ✗ ✗ ✗

Is it bad to be mad?

Anger.
What else causes enraged people to blow their tops, their fuses—even their stacks? Or makes furious teachers flip their lids, fly off the handle, and hit the ceiling? Or prompts hopping mad parents to bite off our heads, get on our backs, and jump down our throats?

Anger. What else can get us hot under the collar, make our blood boil, or even cause us to explode?

Ticked off? Mad as a hornet? Then the next few pages are for you!

"An angry man stirs up dissension, and a hot-tempered one commits many sins" (Proverbs 29:22).

Derrick has had a bad day. Now, after school, he's out in the garage throwing darts with Bill.

Bill has had a good day. He's being obnoxious, giving Derrick a hard time, getting on his nerves.

The more Bill messes with Derrick, the madder Derrick gets. Suddenly Derrick whirls around with eyes blazing. As he yells, "I told you to shut up!" he fires a dart right into Bill's thigh!

It's dangerous to get *angerous!*

Look It Up: Anger is a dangerous emotion that often has devastating results.

• Angry words can cause emotional damage. "The tongue also is a fire, a world of evil among the parts of the body. It corrupts the whole person, sets the whole course of his life on fire, and is itself set on fire by hell. . . . No man can tame the tongue. It is a restless evil, full of deadly poison" (James 3:6, 8).

• Angry thoughts can lead to bitterness and hate (2 Samuel 13).

• Angry actions can culminate in murder (Genesis 4:3-8).

Think It Through: Anger has other negative side effects too. According to Christian psychiatrists Paul D. Meier and Frank B. Minirth, "Pent-up anger is the root of nearly all clinical depression."

Add that statement to the one we read earlier this month—that a large number of patients in mental hospitals are there due to guilt. Then realize: If everyone would follow what God says about anger and guilt, a lot of counselors would be out of work!

Work It Out: Is anger on the verge of ruining your life? Take steps now to deal with your passionate emotions.

1. Pray. You may not feel like talking to God, but He wants to hear from you—even when you're furious. Verbalizing your feelings will help to calm you.

2. Sit down with an older, more mature Christian and ask for advice.

3. Choose to forgive the person(s) who have offended you. You cannot control hurt feelings or erase a painful memory, but by an act of your will you can decide not to hold something against another person.

Nail It Down: Read Matthew 5:21-22.

✱✱✱✱✱✱✱ ONE ANGER ✱✱✱✱✱✱✱

"A hhhhhh!" Bill screams through clenched teeth, grabbing his leg in pain. "What are you—crazy?"

Derrick's temporary rage has given way to guilt. "I'm sorry, man. Are you okay?"

After no response, Derrick mumbles, "Bill, I don't know what makes me explode like that. I'm really sorry—I mean it."

Finally Bill shakes his head. "No hard feelings. But, hey, how else are people supposed to know they're getting on your nerves unless you tell 'em? Man, you're gonna kill somebody if you don't learn to express yourself."

How to be good and angry

Look It Up: Bill's response is an excellent example of how to handle anger. Was he angry at being the target of a hostile dart? (What do you think?) Did he feel like retaliating? (Absolutely.) Could he have harbored a grudge against his explosive friend? (Sure, and lots of people would have.)

He didn't do any of those things. Instead he practiced the truth contained in this verse: "'In your anger do not sin': Do not let the sun go down while you are still angry, and do not give the devil a foothold" (Ephesians 4:26-27).

Think It Through: According to that verse, is it possible to be angry without sinning?

What are some occasions when anger might not be wrong?

How long should you wait before you deal with your anger?

What happens if you don't quickly resolve hostile situations?

Work It Out: Angry? Then it's time for a little R & R.

1. Remember that angry feelings aren't necessarily wrong. (You don't always have to feel bad about feeling mad.)

2. React correctly. Angry feelings must be dealt with quickly and completely. (You do need to resolve hostile situations as they occur. Don't wait! Is there someone you need to phone or visit? Do it today. . . or you'll give the devil a foothold in your life!)

Nail It Down: Even Jesus got angry—see Mark 3:1-5 and John 2:13-17.

Pray About It: _____

Derrick gives Bill a dirty look. "Oh, fine! So now I'm gonna get another lecture about learning to express my feelings? That's great. Look, Bill, I said I'm sorry, okay? So just lay off all the psychoanalysis!"

Bill is shocked. "Derrick! Lighten up! I wasn't attacking you. I just made a simple suggestion. You're schizophrenic! You're like Dr. Jekyll and Mr. Hyde!"

With that Bill turns and walks out of the garage, leaving Derrick leaning against the workbench, a bloody dart in his hand.

Angry for all the wrong reasons

Look It Up: We may get angry for any number of wrong reasons.
- When our pride has been wounded (Numbers 22:24-29)
- When we see in others sins that have also taken root in us (Genesis 38:11-26)
- When we witness God's goodness and mercy to "sinners" (Jonah 3:10–4:4; Luke 15:28-32)
- When we are confronted in our sins—"Whoever corrects a mocker invites insult; whoever rebukes a wicked man incurs abuse. Do not rebuke a mocker or he will hate you; rebuke a wise man and he will love you" (Proverbs 9:7-8).

Think It Through: Do you ever get angry at God? "How could God let this happen to me?" That's a common reaction, especially when people lose a loved one.

Unfortunately, anger at God is always inappropriate. (What right do we have to be angry with a heavenly Father who is always completely good and loving? See Romans 9:20-21.)

Fortunately, God is patient when grieving people question His goodness.

Work It Out: Are you guilty of inappropriate anger? Have you been hostile for any of the wrong reasons?

If so, you might pray like this:

"Father, I know that it's not necessarily a sin to be angry, but it is a sin to be angry for the wrong reasons. Forgive me for getting so upset when _____. Help me to have a more Christlike attitude in the future. Thanks for loving me in spite of what I do. Amen."

Nail It Down: Think hard about the question in Galatians 4:16. How do you respond when someone tells you the truth?

✱ ✱ ✱ ✱ ✱ ✱ ✱ THREE **ANGER** ✱ ✱ ✱ ✱ ✱ ✱ ✱ ✱

As Randy is walking down the hall, one of his "friends" sticks out a leg. Randy stumbles. Everybody laughs. Randy's response is to _____ .

• Cynthia's mom takes on the attitude of a prosecuting attorney. "You went to see Keith last night, didn't you? You ignored what your father and I told you, didn't you?" Cynthia is innocent of the charges, but her mom isn't listening. Cynthia reacts by _____ .

• Raymond spreads a big lie (a very damaging lie) about Marcus. Marcus responds by _____ .

Stopping wrath in its tracks

Look It Up: God's Word gives us a lot of good advice for overcoming anger in our lives.

1. Avoid hostile people when possible. "Do not make friends with a hot-tempered man, do not associate with one easily angered, or you may learn his ways and get yourself ensnared" (Proverbs 22:24-25).

2. Choose to overlook minor irritations. "A man's wisdom gives him patience; it is to his glory to overlook an offense" (Proverbs 19:11).

3. Refuse to respond angrily to a furious person (Proverbs 15:1).

4. Think before you react. "Do not be quickly provoked in your spirit, for anger resides in the lap of fools" (Ecclesiastes 7:9).

Think It Through: U.S. President Thomas Jefferson is reported to have said, "When angry, count to ten before you speak; if very angry, count to a hundred."

Is that good advice? Does such an approach work?

How do you react when you feel yourself getting angry? Is your method of dealing with anger a successful one?

Work It Out: Fill in the blanks in the stories according to how the typical teenager at your school might respond. Then complete the sentences according to how you would respond in each situation.

Think about the people you'll see and the places you'll be during the next 24 hours. What situations will you face that have the potential to become hostile? Pray about each one, asking God to give you His patience and love. Spend five minutes meditating on Ephesians 4:31-32.

Nail It Down: Read Proverbs 17:14 and James 1:19-20.

Pray About It:

✗ ✗ ✗ ✗ ✗ ✗ FOUR

The discussion about God in Mrs. Garcia's Sunday school class last week went something like this.

Tony: "I don't like to think of God like that. I can't accept that He would get angry and be full of wrath and stuff."

Alfredo: "Yeah, I see Him as more loving. You know, 'God is love.'"

Jose: "That's exactly why I don't believe in hell! Because if God is good, I can't imagine that He could send people to burn forever."

The real and awful anger of God

Look It Up: The guys are right about God being loving and good. But we mustn't distort His character. The Bible also makes it clear that sin makes God angry.

• "But the Israelites acted unfaithfully. . . . So the Lord's anger burned against Israel" (Joshua 7:1).

• "But for those who are self-seeking and who reject the truth and follow evil, there will be wrath and anger" (Romans 2:8).

• "Let no one deceive you with empty words, for because of such things God's wrath comes on those who are disobedient" (Ephesians 5:6).

Think It Through: A Christian teenager gets messed up and sins "bigtime" (pregnancy, drugs, stealing). Does this mean God is about to explode in judgment? Will He pour out His fury on such a wayward teen?

No. God's wrath was satisfied in the death of Jesus Christ (1 John 2:2). Christians must realize, however, that the consequences of sin go on and that God does discipline His children.

On the other hand, people who reject Christ will one day stand before an angry God!

Work It Out: Let the fact of God's anger prompt you to lead your non-Christian friends and relatives to Christ.
1. Pray for their salvation.
2. Live a consistent life and earn their respect.
3. Without being pushy, try to initiate conversations about spiritual matters.
4. Invite them to special evangelistic programs at your church.
5. Introduce them to mature, committed Christians.

Nail It Down: Read more about God's anger in Psalm 2. On Saturday, consider Romans 1:18. On Sunday, reflect on John 3:36.

✱✱✱✱✱✱✱ FIVE ANGER ✱✱✱✱✱✱✱✱

▲ ▲ ▲ ▲ CAREER ▲ ▲ ▲ ▲ ▲ ▲
Much more than a paycheck

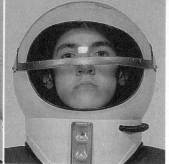

"It is the LORD your God you must follow, and him you must revere. Keep his commands and obey him; serve him and hold fast to him" (Deuteronomy 13:4).

Ask a little kid, "What do you want to be when you grow up?" and you'll get an earful. To a child, no other question is quite as exciting—unless maybe it's the old reliable, "How old are you?"

Well, the point is this: You're not a little kid anymore. You're pretty much grown up now. And it's past time to begin thinking about what you were created to do.

▲ ▲ ▲ ▲ ▲ ▲ ▲ ▲ ▲ ▲ ▲ ▲ ▲ ▲ ▲

The senior class has graduated, and its members are excitedly getting on with their lives: Some are preparing for college, others are starting a variety of jobs, and a handful will soon begin careers in the military.

All this commotion has a few members of the next year's class thinking seriously about their lives after high school.

"Do you know what you want to do, Chuck?"

"Who, me? Are you kidding? I don't even know what I'm doing next weekend—much less for the rest of my life!"

"What should I do with my life?"

Look It Up: The bad news first: The Bible does not give specific directions about careers. It doesn't, for example, say, "God's will for Thomas Jones is a career in aviation." However, it does give a number of foundational principles which ought to shape our thinking in this area. A chosen career should:

1. Bring glory to God (1 Corinthians 10:31).
2. Advance the kingdom of God. "But seek first his kingdom and his righteousness, and all these things will be given to you as well" (Matthew 6:33).
3. Enable us to use our God-given abilities in serving others. "Each one should use whatever gift he has received to serve others, faithfully administering God's grace in its various forms" (1 Peter 4:10).

Think It Through: Choosing a career is more than finding a job and collecting a paycheck. It involves discovering your interests, gifts, and skills, and then finding out where you fit in the world as a servant of God and other people.

Ponder these questions:
• What is my purpose in life?
• What was I created to do?
• What contribution do I want to make to the world?

Work It Out: Begin your week-long study of this important topic with this prayer:

"Dear God, I want so much for my life to count. As I study Biblical principles this week, begin to reveal to me Your purpose for my life. In Jesus' name I pray. Amen."

Nail It Down: How (if at all) should the command of Acts 1:8 affect your career decision?

▲▲▲▲▲▲▲ ONE **CAREER** ▲▲▲▲▲▲▲

Sitting around after Bible study, some members of the senior class are talking with Jeff, their youth leader, about an upcoming career conference.

"I hope the conference gives me some direction, because I don't know what to do. I keep hearing all this stuff about being 'called by God.' But what does that mean? I've never heard God speak out loud to me! Yet Larry is going off to Bible college in the fall because he says he's been 'called to preach.'"

"Do you believe in that, Jeff? Were you called by God?"

Don't trip and fall over your call!

Look It Up: "When I read the Bible," Jeff responds, "I see some individuals who were summoned by God in dramatic ways. Take Abraham for instance. God suddenly spoke to him and said: 'Leave your country, your people and your father's household and go to the land I will show you' (Genesis 12:1).

"Others were steered by God in less dramatic ways. In the Book of Esther, there is no mention of anyone hearing God's call. In fact, God is never even mentioned! Yet, it's clear that He's behind the scenes protecting and guiding His people.

"If you ask me, I think God sometimes speaks to our hearts, impressing us to do certain things. Other times He guides us through events and circumstances."

Think It Through: Do you know that you have been called to be a saint (Romans 1:7); to be like Christ (Romans 8:28-30); to live in peace (1 Corinthians 7:15); to be free (Galatians 5:13); and to live a holy life (1 Thessalonians 4:7)?

Work It Out: How can you hear the call of God? By exposing yourself to His Word and to His world.

Read newspapers, news magazines and missionary prayer letters. Watch films and documentaries that highlight needs at home and abroad. Sign up for a short-term missionary project.

As you prayerfully grapple with the needs of the world and as you come face to face with human suffering, you very well may sense God leading you (or calling you) in a particular direction.

Nail It Down: Don't forget God's call to live "a life of love"— Ephesians 5:1-2.

Pray About It:

▲▲▲▲▲ TWO

Let's listen to one of the career counselors at the Career Conference:

"And so Mark was making a lot of money. He had a great career. But . . . he was also extremely miserable! He came to see me. 'I hate my job!' he announced. 'I only went into this type of work because everyone told me that's where I'd make the bucks.'

"I said to him, 'Mark, forget the money for a minute and tell me this: If you could do any job, anything in the world, what kind of work would you find satisfying?'"

(Continued next column)

Making money isn't always funny!

"He thought for a minute and said, 'I've always liked math . . . and I've always enjoyed high school students. I guess maybe I think it would be fun to be a high school math teacher.'

"'Then go for it!' I told him.

"Guess what? He did! Mark went back to college and is now a high school math teacher. He makes about half as much money as he made before, but he's about ten times more fulfilled!"

Look It Up: When thinking about careers, don't let money dominate your thinking! If anything, money brings headaches—not happiness:

"People who want to get rich fall into temptation and a trap and into many foolish and harmful desires that plunge men into ruin and destruction" (1 Timothy 6:9).

That's a pretty straightforward warning, isn't it?

Think It Through: In the 1960s, a majority of the college freshmen polled wanted careers in helping others. Only a few said their desire was to make a lot of money.

Similar polls today reveal just the opposite. Only a small percentage are seeking careers in which they can serve mankind. Most want vocations that will bring them wealth.

How would you answer if asked you about your career plans? How should a Christian respond?

Work It Out: Spend 20 or 30 minutes thinking about the same question that the career counselor asked Mark. Make a list of the different careers that you would find exciting and fulfilling.

Then remember: When we are walking with God, He gives us the desires of our hearts (Psalm 37:3-5)!

Nail It Down: Read 1 Timothy 6:10.

▲ ▲ ▲ ▲ ▲ ▲ **THREE CAREER** ▲ ▲ ▲ ▲ ▲ ▲

W asn't that great!"

"You mean Jeff's talk on career myths?"

"Yeah. I've been so worried thinking, 'What if I get stuck in the wrong career for the rest of my life?' It freed me up to realize that vocational choices don't have to be permanent. It's okay to change."

"What helped me was realizing that I don't have to wait for some dramatic call from God. God may lead me to the right career through everyday circumstances and plain old common sense."

Foolish fallacies we need to forget!

Look It Up: Consider two more fallacies concerning Christians and careers.

1. *Only a few careers are suitable for Christians.*

This statement cannot be supported by Scripture. With the exception of a few "occupations" that are inherently wrong, most are open to believers.

2. *The best careers for Christians are those in "full-time Christian service." All others are second class.*

This claim ignores the truth that "the earth is the LORD's and everything in it" (Psalm 24:1) and that even "nonspiritual" activities like eating and drinking (and we might add working) can bring glory to God (1 Corinthians 10:31).

Think It Through: If being a full-time Christian worker is the highest form of spirituality:

a. Why did Jesus wait 30 years to begin His public ministry?

b. Why did so many of God's people in the Bible have secular vocations?

Work It Out: Talk to your youth leader about hosting a Career Conference.

• Include both high school and college students.

• Schedule the event over a couple of evenings or on a Saturday.

• Invite special speakers, vocational experts, and career counselors.

• Set up information booths and provide plenty of time for interaction.

Such an event would provide a great outreach to the community, and you might even discover your own career!

Nail It Down: Whatever the career, one must remember Colossians 3:23.

Pray About It:

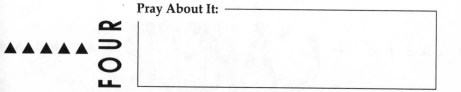

▲ ▲ ▲ ▲ ▲ F O U R

As Marcy sits at the career conference staring at dozens of brochures and handouts listing hundreds of careers available to her, she gets more and more depressed.

"How am I supposed to know what to do?" she moans. "It's too confusing! There are too many options."

Just then, Jeff walks up with a big smile on his face. "Need some help?"

"Please!"

Our desires— a divine design

Look It Up: Scripture gives us excellent principles to use in choosing a career:

1. Examine your own strengths and desires (Galatians 6:4).

2. Get wise counsel (Proverbs 12:15).

3. Carefully consider God's claims on your life (1 Corinthians 6:19-20).

Think It Through: Mentally fill in this blank with several possible options: "I would make a good _____ ."

How do you think your friends and relatives would finish that statement about you?

Work It Out: Take this short career aptitude quiz.

1. What really excites and motivates me is: (a) meeting requirements; (b) overcoming obstacles; (c) serving and helping people; (d) building and developing things; (e) gaining recognition and awards.

2. The abilities I have and want to use are: (a) designing and creating; (b) investigating and negotiating; (c) experimenting and evaluating; (d) speaking and motivating; (e) operating and maintaining.

3. I enjoy: (a) numbers; (b) details; (c) methods and solutions; (d) people; (e) mechanical things.

4. I work best: (a) in competitive environments; (b) in structured, defined situations; (c) in unstructured situations; (d) on projects with clear beginnings and endings; (e) in solving problems.

5. I see myself as: (a) a leader; (b) an independent worker; (c) a team player; (d) an influencer; (e) a self-motivated manager.

Discuss the results with your parents, youth leader, and/or school guidance counselor.

Nail It Down: Read Proverbs 15:22. On Saturday, memorize Colossians 3:2. On Sunday, add Colossians 3:17 to your thinking about careers.

▲▲▲▲▲▲ FIVE **CAREER** ▲▲▲▲▲▲

FEELINGS
Emotions in motion

In every group of people—shoppers at the mall, workers on the job, commuters sitting in traffic—there is a wide variety of emotions.

Some individuals are excited. Others feel depressed. A few are wrestling with anger.

Hostility, nostalgia, loneliness—just name an emotion, and chances are good that someone you know is experiencing it right now.

That's why the Old Testament Psalms are so great. There's a psalm for you—whatever your mood!

"To you I call, O LORD my Rock; do not turn a deaf ear to me" (Psalm 28:1).

Leslie runs upstairs to her room and collapses onto the bed.

Sobbing, she reflects on her awful day.

• Right after her devotional time this morning, Leslie learned that her boyfriend Steve has been dating someone else.

• At the pool this afternoon, two of Leslie's friends were making some vulgar remarks about each guy's physique.

•When Leslie confronted Steve tonight, he got furious and yelled, "Don't act so innocent! I heard you were checking out all the guys at the pool today."

"Help, Lord! I'm all alone."

Look It Up: Everyone who has ever tried to live for God in this really gross world can relate to the cry of King David in Psalm 12: "Help, LORD, for the godly are no more; the faithful have vanished from among men. Everyone lies to his neighbor; their flattering lips speak with deception. . . . The wicked freely strut about when what is vile is honored among men" (vv. 1-2, 8).

Walking with God often results in feelings of loneliness!

Think It Through: Do you feel all alone in your struggle to live a righteous life? Does it make you sad when your Christian friends act like non-Christians? How would you feel if you were in Leslie's situation?

If you're honest, can you relate more to David (the lone, faithful believer), or are you more like the people he writes about (the corrupt masses)?

Work It Out: Notice in Psalm 12 how David responded when he began feeling that he was the only committed believer around.

1. He cried out to God (vv. 1-2).
2. He prayed for truth to win out (v. 3).
3. He remembered the promises of God's Word (vv. 5-6).
4. He expressed his confidence in God (v. 7).

If you're feeling all alone as you try to live for God in a godless society, do what David did. Spend a few minutes alone with God and His Word. Concentrate especially on step three.

Nail It Down: Read all of Psalm 12.

◆◆◆◆◆◆◆◆◆ ONE FEELINGS ◆◆◆◆◆◆◆◆◆

Marcus is a 16-year-old kid with a past.

For three years he ran with a gang. He sold drugs, he did drugs, he committed robbery. Then he met Jesus Christ. Leaving his wild life behind, Marcus devoted himself completely to God.

Now Marcus is trying to finish high school and talks of becoming a minister.

But this morning, some older drug dealers came around the neighborhood looking for Marcus. They say he still owes them money. And they looked pretty angry.

"Help, Lord! I'm scared."

Look It Up: People in trouble can find great comfort in Psalm 40. There King David wrote: "I waited patiently for the LORD; he turned to me and heard my cry. He lifted me out of the slimy pit, out of the mud and mire; he set my feet on a rock and gave me a firm place to stand" (vv. 1-2).

Then, after remembering God's goodness to him, David began to pray urgently about problems in the present: "For troubles without number surround me; my sins have overtaken me, and I cannot see. They are more than the hairs of my head, and my heart fails within me. Be pleased, O LORD, to save me" (vv. 12-13).

Think It Through: Maybe you can't relate to the problems facing Marcus, but are you facing a troubling situation? (A bad home environment? A possible move? Threats from someone at school?)

How do you normally respond when you feel overwhelmed by frightening circumstances? Do you panic. . . or do you pray?

Work It Out: First, scan Psalm 40:1-8 and make a note of each thing God did for the troubled psalmist.

Second, reflect on all the good things God has done for you.

Third, make a list of the troubles you are facing now. Using Psalm 40:9-17 as your guide, pray about each problem, and ask God to intervene in your life.

Fourth, do something today to help someone else who is in trouble. A kind word, a note, a phone call—these thoughtful gestures will not only mean a lot to a friend, but they will also help get your mind off your own problems.

Nail It Down: Memorize Psalm 40:8 and read Psalm 70.

Pray About It:

◆◆◆◆◆◆◆◆ T W O

Fifteen-year-old Rachel is lying in a girl's bunkhouse at a missionary compound in Haiti. In the last five days she has witnessed abject poverty (both material and spiritual). She has seen people wracked by sickness (of both body and soul). This afternoon she visited an orphanage where dozens of kids have bloated bellies and bleak futures.

As she listens to the chorus of crickets outside, she prays, "God, why are you so good to me? Why was I born into a Christian family, a loving home with so many material blessings?"

"Why are you so good to me, Lord?"

Look It Up: Certain circumstances create strong feelings of gratitude within us. Sometimes we may even feel like falling on our faces and thanking God for how good He has been to us.

Many of the psalms were written during such times when God's people were overcome by strong feelings of thanksgiving, but consider just one— Psalm 65.

"Praise awaits you, O God, in Zion; to you our vows will be fulfilled. . . . When we were overwhelmed by sins, you atoned for our transgressions. Blessed are those you choose and bring near to live in your courts! We are filled with the good things of your house, of your holy temple. . . . The streams of God are filled with water to provide the people with grain, for so you have ordained it" (vv. 1, 3-4, 9).

Think It Through: When was the last time you found yourself overwhelmed by feelings like the ones Rachel felt on her mission trip?

Why do you think God has so abundantly blessed this nation and the Christians in this nation?

What blessings are you most grateful for?

Work It Out: Thanksgiving is still five months away, but that doesn't mean you have to wait to express your thanks to God.

Make a list of the things you are grateful for. Then spend some time telling God you appreciate what He has done.

(Guess what? Even if you don't feel thankful right now, chances are you will sense feelings of gratitude in your heart by the time you finish this exercise!)

Nail It Down: Read all of Psalm 65.

❖❖❖❖❖❖❖❖ THREE **FEELINGS** ❖❖❖❖❖❖❖

Ron is on the verge of going crazy. He graduated from high school a few weeks ago, and now he doesn't have a clue about what to do next.

Should he go to the junior college near his hometown? Should he join the army along with some of his high school buddies? Should he go to work immediately and begin working his way up the career ladder? Did God really call him into the ministry when he was 15, or was he just being emotional at that retreat?

"Oh, Lord," Ron prays, "What should I do? I'm so confused!"

"Oh, Lord, please direct me!"

Look It Up: Most of us can relate to feelings of confusion and to Ron's question, "Lord, what do You want me to do?" Perhaps that's a reason Psalm 119 is a favorite for so many people.

"Teach me, O LORD, to follow your decrees; then I will keep them to the end. Give me understanding, and I will keep your law and obey it with all my heart. Direct me in the path of your commands, for there I find delight. Turn my heart toward your statutes and not toward selfish gain. Turn my eyes away from worthless things; preserve my life according to your word" (vv. 33-37).

The message? God's Word can give us real direction and purpose in life!

Think It Through: Do you feel confused right now about your direction in life? According to Psalm 119, where is the best guidance found?

What would you counsel Ron to do if he came to you for advice?

Work It Out: Confused about making a decision?
1. Pray for wisdom (Philippians 4:6-7).
2. Read and study God's Word (see below).
3. Seek the counsel of mature Christians (Proverbs 15:22) who know and love you.
4. Look for God's leading in your circumstances (Romans 8:28).
5. Use your common sense, your transformed reason (Romans 12:2).
6. Follow the course of action that brings peace to your spirit (Colossians 3:15).

Nail It Down: Before going to sleep tonight, carefully read all 176 verses of Psalm 119.

Pray About It:

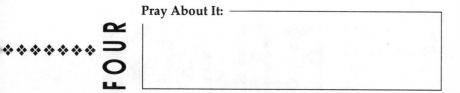

❖❖❖❖❖❖❖ FOUR

97

When Donna heard about a youth group weekend retreat at a conference center up in the mountains she thought, "Perfect! That's exactly what I need. A chance to get away and get my act together. Since my relationship with God has been practically nonexistent the last few weeks, this'll be a great opportunity to rest and reflect and get refreshed."

She signed up immediately.

On Sunday night, after the retreat was over, Donna felt even more pooped than she did before she left town on Friday afternoon!

"Lord, I feel so weary!"

Look It Up: We are frenzied, wild-and-crazy, never-sit-still, always-in-motion people who live in a hectic, action-packed, chaotic culture. No wonder we feel so worn out all the time! Listen to the psalmist.

"I remember the days of long ago; I meditate on all your works and consider what your hands have done. I spread out my hands to you; my soul thirsts for you like a parched land. Answer me quickly, O LORD; my spirit faints with longing. Do not hide your face from me or I will be like those who go down to the pit" (Psalm 143:5-7).

When was the last time you took time for such reflection?

Think It Through: If retreats are supposed to be times of solitude and rest, why do most people who go on them come home exhausted?

What would happen if your church or youth group had a retreat with no games or scheduled activities—just time for reading God's Word, quiet meditation, and sleeping? What if there was a rule that no one could talk during the entire weekend—except to God? Would anyone sign up? Would you?

Work It Out: Feeling spiritually dry and blah?

Take your own personal retreat. Grab your Bible, a notebook, a pen, and find a peaceful place. Spend a whole morning (nine to noon) talking to God, praising Him, reading His Word, and singing praises.

Personal retreats are refreshing and fun! You may find that three hours are too short!

Nail It Down: Read Psalm 23 today. On Saturday, check out Psalm 103. Then on Sunday, think about the message of Psalm 145.

FIVE FEELINGS

THE BIGGEST
BIBLE MESSES

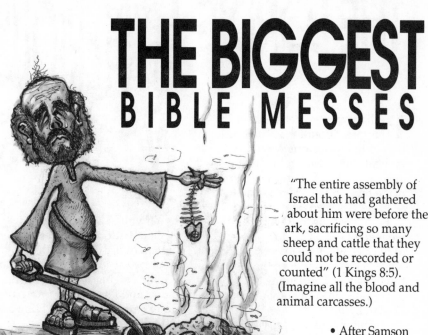

"The entire assembly of Israel that had gathered about him were before the ark, sacrificing so many sheep and cattle that they could not be recorded or counted" (1 Kings 8:5). (Imagine all the blood and animal carcasses.)

I magine being on the clean-up crew in these situations!

• With Noah on the Ark, full of animals, for over a year (Genesis 7:11–8:19). (Think about the implications of that!)

• After the plague of frogs in Egypt. When Moses finally asked God to stop the plague, the billions and billions of frogs "died in the houses, in the courtyards and in the fields. They were piled into heaps, and the land reeked of them" (Exodus 8:13-14).

• After King Solomon brought the ark of God (not Noah's) to Jerusalem,

• After Samson "brought down the house" (actually a pagan temple) on top of himself and 3,000 Philistines (Judges 16:23-30).

• The morning after the angel of the Lord put to death 185,000 Assyrians who were encamped around Judah and intent on taking Jerusalem (2 Kings 19:35-36).

•After Paul's preaching of the gospel started riots in Thessalonica, Ephesus, and Jerusalem (Acts 17–21).

•During the Tribulation when a third of the earth will burn up and a third of the creatures in the sea will die (Revelation 8:7-9).

THE LORD'S MYSTERIOUS WAYS

Perhaps you've heard the famous quotation, "The Lord moves in mysterious ways." A biblical statement, right? Well, yes and no. You won't find that verse in the Bible. But the *idea* behind that sentiment is seen on every page.

From Genesis to Revelation, we read about a Creator who seldom does what we expect, a God who, in fact, often does the very things we *least* anticipate.

He puts on skin and becomes a human being.

He enters our world without any fanfare. No live television, no press conferences, no schmoozing with society's celebrities at some glitzy hotel in New York. Instead, when we first meet Him, He is an infant—lying helplessly in a slop bin in a ramshackle shed in Bethlehem, Israel.

Thirty years later, He criticizes the religious leaders, and chooses instead to hang out with society's losers. He selects as sidekicks, not a bunch of clean-cut Christian clones, but 12 rugged, opinionated individuals.

Then he teaches them outrageous ideas like:

• "If you want to be a leader, become a servant."

• "If you want to really live, you first have·to die."

• "If you believe in me and associate with me, you will suffer."

He demonstrates His divine power by raising a dead man and calming a raging sea. Then He turns around and lets a small group of soldiers arrest Him, beat Him, and kill Him.

Next thing you know, He's alive again. And just when it looks like He might finally get the bad guys, He goes back up to heaven.

And here we are, waiting for Him to return.

To say that "the Lord moves in mysterious ways" means this: As soon as we try to put God in a box, He shatters all our categories. He is unpredictable, yet always faithful; uncontrollable, but never out of control; and surprising, but never contradictory.

What is God going to do next—in the world or in your life? There's no telling. Maybe that's why the apostle Paul wrote, *"Now to him who is able to do immeasurably more than all we ask or imagine . . . to him be glory!"* (Ephesians 3:20-21).

HONESTY
"Cross my heart . . ."

What if we could show you how to
- build a better reputation,
- have better relationships at home and with friends,
- enjoy peace of mind,
- please God, and
- enjoy God's blessings both now and forever?

Would you be interested? (Here's a hint: The secret is written out in big, bold letters at the top of this page.)

"Do not lie to each other" (Colossians 3:9).

Lies, lies, and more lies!

Karen tells her mom, "But I did! I got home at 11:00, I promise!" (More like 11:20 actually.)

Bill urges Neil, "C'mon, tell me the big secret. I promise I won't breathe a word of it to anyone else." (Funny how six people knew Neil's news the next day.)

Stacey: "Dad, can I use your car to go to the library tonight?" (When you think about it, Dale's house is sort of like a library. I mean, it's a building—and it does have a few books inside.)

Fakes, frauds, and falsehoods!

Look It Up: About the devil, Jesus said, "He was a murderer from the beginning, not holding to the truth, for there is no truth in him. When he lies, he speaks his native language, for he is a liar and the father of lies" (John 8:44).

Since the master deceiver is also the god of this world (2 Corinthians 4:4), it's not surprising that we live in a society that is built on satanic subterfuge and filled with devilish deceit.

No wonder the psalmist cried, "All men are liars" (Psalm 116:11).

No wonder the Prophet Jeremiah wailed, "Friend deceives friend, and no one speaks the truth. They have taught their tongues to lie; they weary themselves with sinning" (Jeremiah 9:5).

Think It Through: Have you lied in the last two days? Why? What was so scary about telling the truth that you felt you had to lie? What does lying accomplish? If you haven't told a lie, have you recently done something that was dishonest or deceitful?

How do you feel when you are caught in a lie?

Have you been lied to recently? How did you feel when you discovered that you had been duped?

Work It Out: Dishonesty only advances the cause of Satan. And people who lie are really rejecting God (since He is the source of all truth).

Say no to that kind of lifestyle. Pray this Bible verse: "Keep falsehood and lies far from me" (Proverbs 30:8).

Think about the situations cited at the beginning of this page. How would you react in each one? How should you react?

Nail It Down: Satan may be a liar, but God is 100 percent honest! Read Psalm 31:5 and Titus 1:2.

• • • • • • • ONE **HONESTY** • • • • • • •

At the mall with some friends, Carl decides he wants a slice of pizza. Problem is he has no money.

"Hey, Steve, can you lend me a couple of bucks?"

"I lend you money all the time and never get it back."

"C'mon, man. I'm starving! I'll pay you back tomorrow when I get my allowance."

"That's what you always say."

"Do you want a letter from my attorney? I said I'll pay you back!"

"Oh, all right," Steve huffs, reaching into his wallet.

Bet you can guess the rest of that story.

Dishonesty is disastrous!

Look It Up: What's wrong with lying?
• "The LORD detests lying lips, but he delights in men who are truthful" (Proverbs 12:22).
• "A false witness will not go unpunished, and he who pours out lies will perish" (Proverbs 19:9).
• "A fortune made by a lying tongue is a fleeting vapor and a deadly snare" (Proverbs 21:6).

Think It Through: Sooner or later, liars always get caught. Like the time four guys arrived late for class, telling their teacher, "Um, sorry we're late . . . er, we had a flat tire."

After class she detained the latecomers. "Since you missed our regular class quiz, I'll need to give you a make-up. Take out a sheet of paper and answer this question: Which tire on your car went flat?"

So much for that tall tale! Are your friends honest? Do people consider you a truthful person?

Work It Out: What can you do about lying lips? Plenty!
• Confess to the friend you recently deceived.
• Admit any misleading remarks made to your parents.
• Set the record straight with your boss.
• Tell your brother or sister what really happened.
• Fulfill the promise or pledge that you made earlier in the week.
• Acknowledge those things you did that you claimed you didn't do.

And if others aren't even aware they've been had? Admit your lie and apologize anyway. Better a little embarrassment now, than being caught in your deception later. (Besides, you'll gain a lot of respect!)

Nail It Down: Read Proverbs 6:16-19.

Pray About It:

TWO

Lawrence is dishonest. Not in the sense that he says a lot of false things, but more in the sense that he acts differently around different people.

With his neighborhood buddies he curses like a sailor and drinks like a fish. With his church friends Lawrence talks about Jesus and acts like a model Christian.

To his parents, Lawrence is rude and obnoxious. To his girlfriend's mom, he is polite and considerate.

Lawrence is a chameleon. His life is a lie.

Is your life a giant lie?

Look It Up: A hypocritical lifestyle produces insecurity: "The man of integrity walks securely, but he who takes crooked paths will be found out" (Proverbs 10:9).

But more than just the fear of being discovered, living a lie also results in disaster: "He whose walk is blameless is kept safe, but he whose ways are perverse will suddenly fall" (Proverbs 28:18).

Think It Through: Are you living a lie? Here's how to tell. Consider the reactions (both yours and the person or group described) in each of the following scenarios:
• If your parents found an audio tape of your last heart-to-heart conversation with your best friend
• If your pastor saw a video of your last date
• If your Christian friends saw how you act around your non-Christian friends
• If Jesus walked in on one of your parties
• If your future employer knew everything about your present job performance

Work It Out: Don't be swayed by the crowd. Stand up for the truth—all the time and everywhere you go! That's integrity—being complete or whole. It means being all that you are wherever you are. Acting one way here and another way there shows hypocrisy, not integrity.

Check your life for dishonest habits such as stealing, telling "little white lies," exaggerating, shading the truth, being two-faced, cheating, being fake, pretending to be nice, acting like things are okay when they aren't, bragging, or not practicing what you preach in some other way.

When you find an inconsistency, work with God on rooting it out of your life!

Nail It Down: See Proverbs 14:11 and Proverbs 28:6.

THREE **HONESTY**

When Betty walks through the family room, her brother Kelly starts laughing. "Nice outfit ... you look like Ronald McDonald."

"Who asked you?"

"Nobody, but I thought you'd like to know that you look like a clown. You're not going out are you?"

"Shut up, jerk!" Betty snaps, hurling a pillow.

The projectile misses Kelly and sends a crystal lamp crashing to the floor.

Mrs. Harelson rushes in demanding, "Who broke my favorite lamp?"

Honesty really *is* the best policy!

Look It Up: Why is honesty such a good idea?
- It pleases God. "The LORD abhors dishonest scales, but accurate weights are his delight" (Proverbs 11:1).
- Honesty helps rather than hurts us. "An evil man is trapped by his sinful talk, but a righteous man escapes trouble" (Proverbs 12:13).
- Wise people appreciate hearing the truth. "He who rebukes a man will in the end gain more favor" (Proverbs 28:23).

Think It Through: Should we say anything and everything we think? Is that what honesty means? ("Your breath smells like sewage!" or "You look horrible. Did someone hit you with a wet cat or something?")

No. Honesty must always be balanced by sensitivity and love. It's never right to tactlessly blast someone. We must carefully choose our words and pray for wisdom before confronting another.

How would you react if you were in Betty's or Kelly's shoes? How should you respond?

Work It Out: Become a reliable, trustworthy person. Establish a reputation for honesty. How?

1. Don't promise what you can't deliver. (If you make a commitment, keep it!)
2. Don't say things that you don't mean. (Mean what you say and say what you mean.)
3. Give credit where credit is due. (Don't steal someone else's glory!)
4. Take the blame when you are at fault. (No finger pointing, no excuses.)

Nail It Down: Notice the response of those in authority to individuals who are honest— Proverbs 16:13.

Pray About It:

FOUR

• • • • • • • •

David has had a rotten week. At a pool party three nights ago some "friends" pulled the back of his swimsuit down—right in front of a group of girls. Then last night a bunch of people went to a nearby amusement park, and nobody called to invite him.

David feels rejected, left out, lonely, and hurt. Sitting in his room, he starts to pray out loud.

Being an "honest-to-God" Christian

Look It Up: Consider the manner in which certain Bible characters talked with God during difficult times.

• General Joshua, after a stinging military defeat— "Ah, Sovereign LORD, why did you ever bring this people across the Jordan to deliver us into the hands of the Amorites to destroy us?" (Joshua 7:7). In other words, "God, You tricked us! Where are You?"

• Job, when his whole life was falling apart— "Only grant me these two things, O God . . . : Withdraw your hand far from me, and stop frightening me with your terrors" (Job 13:20-21). In other words, "Please God! I can't take it anymore."

• King David, when others were conspiring against him—"Hear me, O God, as I voice my complaint" (Psalm 64:1).

The message of these verses is clear: It's okay to talk openly and honestly with God.

Think It Through: Are you honest with God? Do you tell Him what's really on your mind, or only what you think He wants to hear? Why?

Work It Out: Let one or more of the following phrases launch you into a heart-to-heart talk with God:

1. "God, I feel sad because . . . "
2. "Because of _____ , Lord, I'm really angry and . . . "
3. "Father, I don't understand why . . . "
4. "God, if only You would _____ , then I . . . "
5. "Lord, my biggest worry right now is that . . . "
6. "The one thing that causes me to doubt is . . . "

Nail It Down: Read Moses' frank prayer in Numbers 11:10-15. On Saturday, reflect on Jeremiah's brutal honesty—Jeremiah 12:1-4 and 20:1-18. On Sunday, consider what Proverbs 19:5 says about dishonesty.

FIVE HONESTY

SEX
Playing on the edge of the cliff

In a recent write-in poll, we asked the question, "What topics would you most like to see covered in this book?" An overwhelming number of readers scribbled that ever-popular three-letter word: S-E-X.

So here it is—five pages designed to answer your questions, combat the lies you're being fed, and spare you the bitter heartache that so many teens are experiencing because of this issue.

Believe it or not, the Bible has a lot to say about sex. Apparently the issue is just as important to God as it is to you.

"See that no one is sexually immoral" (Hebrews 12:16).

Katie is reading an article in *Worldly Woman* magazine entitled, "How an Affair Can Save Your Marriage." Suddenly she realizes it's time for her favorite TV talk show. Tuning in, she discovers today's topic: bisexual parents.

At first she thinks, "Yuck!" Afterwards she reasons, "Maybe my views on sex are too closed-minded. After all, we are heading toward the year two thousand."

Revelations for the (sexual) revolution

Look It Up: The so-called sexual revolution is not really new at all. "Alternative lifestyles" have been around for a long time. Notice what God told the nation Israel:

"You must not do as they do in Egypt, where you used to live, and you must not do as they do in the land of Canaan, where I am bringing you. Do not follow their practices. . . . No one is to approach any close relative to have sexual relations. I am the LORD. . . . Do not have sexual relations with your neighbor's wife and defile yourself with her. . . . Do not lie with a man as one lies with a woman; that is detestable. Do not have sexual relations with an animal and defile yourself with it. . . . That is a perversion. Do not defile yourselves in any of these ways, because this is how the nations that I am going to drive out before you became defiled" (Leviticus 18:3, 6, 20, 22-24).

Think It Through: In a few paragraphs, God condemns incest, adultery, homosexuality, and bestiality (sex with animals). All such practices are disgusting to God.

In what ways does our "liberated" society try to make any or all of those behaviors acceptable?

Does the fact that a command is old automatically mean it is no longer appropriate?

Work It Out: Start your week off with this prayer:

"Father, my society is obsessed with sex. Give me wisdom this week. Remind me of what is right and wrong. And grant me the grace to live a pure life in a very impure world. I want my friends (and the world) to see that sex is best when it is reserved for marriage. In Jesus' name. Amen."

Nail It Down: Read the straight scoop on prostitution —Leviticus 19:29; Deuteronomy 23:17-18.

∞ ∞ ∞ ∞ ∞ ∞ ∞ ∞ O N E **SEX** ∞

After her honeymoon with Steve, 23-year-old Paula is talking with some of the girls in her high school Bible study.

"Was it hard to wait? You better believe it! The temptations were incredible, and it would have been so easy to rationalize—'We'll be married in a few days.' But because we held out, we had no reason to feel guilty or weird on our wedding night. Hey, the world may scoff at virginity, but I know a lot of people who wish they had waited. I don't know any who wish they hadn't."

Why it's wisest to wait

Look It Up: After citing the dangers of sex outside of marriage, the writer of Proverbs expounds on the blessings of sex within marriage:

"Drink water from your own cistern, running water from your own well. . . . May your fountain be blessed, and may you rejoice in the wife of your youth. A loving doe, a graceful deer . . . may you ever be captivated by her love. Why be captivated, my son, by an adulteress? Why embrace the bosom of another man's wife? For a man's ways are in full view of the LORD, and he examines all his paths" (Proverbs 5:15, 18-21).

In short, waiting until marriage for sex brings the long-term physical and emotional satisfaction we all long for . . . plus the spiritual benefit of a life that is pleasing to God.

Think It Through: First, consider the following poem that a broken-hearted woman once sent to columnist Ann Landers:

"I met him; I liked him./I liked him; I loved him.
I loved him; I let him./I let him; I lost him."

Second, reflect on this statement: "There is only one first time. Once you give away your virginity, you can never, ever get it back."

Work It Out: Read one of these excellent books on sex:
• *Why Wait?* by Josh McDowell & Dick Day
• *Worth the Wait* by Tim Stafford
• *Handling Your Hormones* by Jim Burns
Maybe you could even get some friends together and do a group study.

Nail It Down: Read Proverbs 5:1-14.

Pray About It:

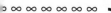

T W O

D ave is
watching
"Wiseguy." This
week's plot is more
of the same—the
main character
cracks another dif-
ficult case and
manages to score
with yet another
beautiful woman.
"What a stud!"
Dave thinks to
himself.

Meanwhile,
his sister Anita is
downstairs reading
a romance novel
and fantasizing.
"Why can't I be
trapped on a desert
island with some-
one like Lance?"

Pleasure now— or pain later?

Look It Up: The Bible warns of the dangers of casual sex: "Do not lust in your heart after her beauty or let her captivate you with her eyes, for the prostitute reduces you to a loaf of bread, and the adulteress preys upon your very life. Can a man scoop fire into his lap without his clothes being burned? Can a man walk on hot coals without his feet being scorched? So is he who sleeps with another man's wife; no one who touches her will go unpunished. . . . A man who commits adultery lacks judgment; whoever does so destroys himself. Blows and disgrace are his lot, and his shame will never be wiped away" (Proverbs 6:25-29, 32-33).

Think It Through: Does sex feel good? Sure, that's the way God made it. But the long-term negative consequences far outweigh any short-term feelings of physical pleasure. Premarital sex
  1. May become addictive
  2. Can expose one to STDs (sexually transmitted diseases) including AIDS
  3. May increase a woman's risk of cervical cancer
  4. Can result in pregnancy
  5. Can lead to a loss of trust in marriage
  6. Often lowers one's self-esteem
  7. Generally creates overpowering feelings of guilt
  8. Always harms one's relationship with God
  Based on this abbreviated list, do you think sex outside of marriage is really "safe"?

Work It Out: Be radical. Declare your nonparticipation in premarital sex. If friends or teachers discuss the subject, make your views known. Memorize the above list, and you will be able to back up your statements with facts. Remember: The more people hear you talk about abstinence, the less "weird" it will seem.

Nail It Down: Read Proverbs 7.

THREE **SEX**

With her high moral standards, Penny Pruitt is known as Penny "Won't do it." Does the teasing hurt?

"Look, they may laugh, but I've seen in their lives what happens when you let your passions get out of control. In our class just this year there have been three abortions . . . not to mention a whole lot of broken hearts. And it's all because of sex. I'm just guarding my heart and trying to control my desires. What's so wrong with that?"

Learn to control your desires!

Look It Up: Nothing! In fact, God tells us to do just that:
"It is God's will that you should be sanctified: that you should avoid sexual immorality; that each of you should learn to control his own body in a way that is holy and honorable, not in passionate lust like the heathen, who do not know God. . . . For God did not call us to be impure, but to live a holy life" (1 Thessalonians 4:3-5, 7).

By the way, if you're looking for a good role model, consider the example of Joseph in Genesis 39.

Think It Through: Everybody wants to know "How far is too far?" Some ask that question with a genuine desire to know God's limits. But some ask it with a selfish motive. They really mean, "What's the most I can possibly get away with?" Which motive is yours?

Whether you are going "too far" can be measured by questions like:
- "Am I aroused to the point of temptation?"
- "Would I be embarrassed for godly friends to witness this?"
- "Does this require a dark, secluded place?"
- "Will this make me or someone else feel guilty?"

Work It Out: Perhaps as you read this, you feel twinges of guilt because you have already gone too far sexually. If that is the case, reflect on God's incredible willingness to forgive. Read Psalms 51 and 103. Meditate on 1 John 1:9.

Then pray, "God, I'm sorry for my sin. I want to know Your forgiveness and cleansing. Thank You for loving me. Give me the strength to turn away from past wrongs. Grant me a fresh start."

Nail It Down: Notice Jesus' loving response to the woman caught in adultery—John 8:1-11.

Pray About It:

∞ ∞ ∞ ∞ ∞ ∞ **FOUR**

Johnny and Angie just ended their relationship. After a year together, their break-up is sad, but not nearly as difficult as it would be if the Central High juniors had been sexually involved.

See, that was a commitment they made from the very start—no messing around! And because they worked hard to keep their relationship pure, they're able to be friends.

Purity in a polluted world

Look It Up: How can you be pure in a polluted world?

1. Fill your mind with pure thoughts (Philippians 4:8), not media garbage.

2. Find pure friends who can encourage you to walk with God (1 Corinthians 5:11; 15:33).

3. Reject the philosophy that says, "Live for the moment!" Remember that today's pleasure very often leads to tomorrow's pain. "Do not be deceived: God cannot be mocked. A man reaps what he sows" (Galatians 6:7).

Think It Through: Circle any items that would encourage sexual purity. Scratch through any activities that might be dangerous:

time alone
praying together
suggestive clothing
watching sexy videos
setting standards
being accountable to someone

Work It Out: Come up with a good response for each of the following stupid lines (we've given you a hint in each case):

• "Real men are sexually active." (So is my dog.)

• "But I want to." (Yeah, and the people in hell want ice water.)

• "I won't get you pregnant." (That's right, because you're not going to touch me.)

• "But you owe me!" (Okay, I'll get you a key chain or something.)

Nail It Down: Read Leviticus 20:10-21. On Saturday, memorize Colossians 3:5-6. On Sunday, compare the fruit of the Holy Spirit (Galatians 5:22-23) with society's self-centered version of sex "whenever I want it."

FIVE **SEX**

TEN DISTINCTIONS
BETWEEN CHRISTIANITY & NEW AGE RELIGION

	THE BIBLE'S VIEW:	THE NEW AGE VIEW:
1. About God	The personal Creator who is holy and distinct from His creation	The impersonal Force which is both good and evil and permeates everything
2. About the universe	Composed of separate objects and people; widespread diversity	All is one; cosmic unity
3. About the location of truth	Revealed by God in the Bible	Found within each person
4. About determining right and wrong	Based on the absolute standards of the Bible	Based on relative, personal, subjective feelings
5. About man	A creature of God who bears the image of God despite his rebellion	A god
6. About mankind's problems	Sinful rebellion against God's holy character	Ignorance of true potential
7. About the solution to mankind's problems	We must repent of sin and trust in the Lord Jesus Christ for salvation	We must each discover our true identity as limitless, divine beings
8. About Jesus Christ	The unique God-man; Lord and Savior of the world	A great guru, or teacher
9. About religion	Only one from God; the rest teach error	The various religions represent the many paths to God
10. About death	Leads to either heaven or hell (resurrection)	Leads to the next life (reincarnation)

FINDING THE LOVE
OF A LIFETIME

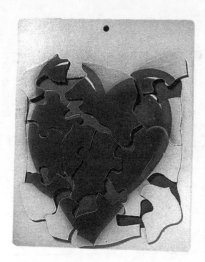

How would you feel if someone knew everything about you—even your deepest, darkest secrets?

If you're like most people, you don't want anyone to know *too much* about you. The fear is that if someone *really* got to know you—including all your faults, embarrassing moments, and hidden sins—they might decide you weren't very likable or worth spending time with.

Guess what? There *is* Someone who knows you. In fact, He knows *everything* about you—the good, the bad, and the ugly. All your thoughts, your dreams, your deepest desires, your highest achievements, your greatest failures. That's kind of scary, isn't it? But . . .

How would you feel if this One who knows you completely —inside and out—also loved you more than you could even imagine—with no strings attached?

It's true. God is the One who knows us, and His response is *love*. Maybe when you hear "God loves you," you wonder, "Why?

Why me?"

God doesn't love you because of who you are or anything you've done. He loves you simply because of who *He* is. It's the way He is. It's His character. His is the purest, most powerful, most perfect form of love there is.

How can having a relationship with the God who knows and loves you affect your life?

When God created you, His purpose was that you might receive His love. It's that simple. God offers His love. He wants you to see your need for it. He wants you to receive it.

When we *do* accept His love, we experience security. No longer do we have to fear what others might think. No longer do we have to wonder if we'll find acceptance. Why? *Because the One who knows us best loves us most!* His perfect love chases fear away and replaces it with freedom.

"But God demonstrates his own love for us in this: While we were still sinners, Christ died for us" (Romans 5:8).

LONELINESS
etting out of solitary confinement

E vangelist Billy Graham says that loneliness is the greatest problem facing humanity today.

Do you agree?

Have you ever felt it—a smothering anxiety that makes you think you just don't matter?

Perhaps you even feel it right now.

"Turn to me and be gracious to me, for I am lonely and afflicted" (Psalm 25:16).

Ron is about to begin his last year at Murphy High. He's a starter on the football team. He has a bunch of friends—even a girlfriend. On top of everything, he's a Christian. But believe it or not, Ron still feels lonely sometimes:

"I don't know . . . it's hard to explain. I mean, I can find people to do stuff with, but nobody is willing to take the time to listen to what I think. Nobody really understands me. I guess you could say I just don't feel very important."

Look at all the lonely people

Look It Up: Loneliness is something all people feel some of the time, and some people feel all of the time. Even some prominent Bible characters wrestled with that awful dilemma of feeling cut off and isolated.

• King David: "Because of all my enemies, I am the utter contempt of my neighbors; I am a dread to my friends—those who see me on the street flee from me. I am forgotten by them as though I were dead; I have become like broken pottery" (Psalm 31:11-12).

• Job (Job 19:13-14)

• The apostle Paul: "At my first defense, no one came to my support, but everyone deserted me" (2 Timothy 4:16).

Think It Through: Let's correct a common misconception: It isn't just homeless people or society's outcasts who feel the sting of loneliness. Albert Einstein reportedly once told a friend, "It is strange to be known so universally and yet be so lonely." And when movie star Joan Crawford died, she was described by one newspaper as "lonely, bitter, reclusive."

Work It Out: What are we saying in all this? It's simple: We live in a world filled with lonely people (you may even be one yourself).

What's the best way to launch ourselves into this important discussion? How about this prayer:

"Father in heaven, I need You right now. Give me insight as I read Your Word this week. Fill my loneliness with Your life. Then use me to bring comfort to other people who face lives of 'solitary confinement.' "

Nail It Down: Read and think about the implications of Genesis 2:18.

▼▼▼▼▼▼ ONE **LONELINESS** ▼▼

Sara has just moved with her family to a new community. She did not want to leave her hometown a month before her long-awaited freshman year at Clark High School, but did anyone bother to consult her? No way!

So on her first day at the new school Sara doesn't know a soul. She feels ignored, stared at, forgotten, insignificant, isolated, left out, ugly, unloved, misunderstood, and abandoned.

In a word, Sara is experiencing loneliness.

Lonely. . . but never alone

Look It Up: Sara *feels* alone. But is she? Not according to the Bible. God's Word tells us that we are never alone. We may have feelings of loneliness, but the fact is that we always have a Friend in the Lord.

• "Can a mother forget the baby at her breast and have no compassion on the child she has borne? Though she may forget, I will not forget you! See, I have engraved you on the palms of my hands" (Isaiah 49:15-16).

• "I will not leave you as orphans; I will come to you" (John 14:18).

• "God has said, 'Never will I leave you; never will I forsake you' " (Hebrews 13:5).

Hey, even when everyone else leaves you or no one else knows you, God is right there, always ready to comfort you. Now that's good news!

Think It Through: Have you ever been in a situation similar to the one Sara is facing? How did you feel at the time? How did you handle it? Did your plan work?

Have any new families moved into your neighborhood this summer? Anyone your age? How could you make that new person feel more welcome?

Work It Out: Are you lonely right now? Don't sit there and have a pity-party! Do something! Take a 15-minute walk—just you and Jesus. Tell Him everything that's on your heart and mind. Yes, He already knows, but telling Him somehow makes things better.

Then softly sing your favorite old hymn or praise chorus and think about the words. (Warning: If you jog and sing at the same time, you need to be in good shape. Otherwise you'll sound like a bagpipe!)

Nail It Down: Consider the last sentence of Matthew 28:20.

Pray About It: —————————————————————

TWO

Last week Frank was in a busy restaurant with a group of friends. Suddenly someone said, "Let's skate!" One by one the guys—under the pretense of going to the restroom—slipped outside without paying their bills.

Soon only Gordon and Frank were left. "C'mon, dude!" Gordon urged. "Let's go before we get caught."

"No way. I'm paying for my dinner. You guys are wrong."

Well, Gordon split, the manager freaked, the police arrived, and now Frank is catching serious heat from his so-called friends.

The loneliness of obedience

Look It Up: Living for God and being obedient to His will often result in loneliness. Consider

• The career of Jeremiah the prophet: "But as soon as Jeremiah finished telling all the people everything the LORD had commanded him to say, the priests, the prophets, and all the people seized him and said, 'You must die!' " (Jeremiah 26:8).

• The words of Christ: "All men will hate you because of me, but he who stands firm to the end will be saved" (Matthew 10:22).

• The experience of Paul: "In fact, everyone who wants to live a godly life in Christ Jesus will be persecuted" (2 Timothy 3:12).

Think It Through: Has obedience to Christ ever cost you anything? Have you ever felt the pain of loneliness because you refused to join others in sin?

What would you have done in Frank's situation?

Work It Out: Determine your response in each of these instances:

1. Friends invite you to a wild celebration (complete with alcohol and without adults to supervise).

2. At the movie theater, everyone in the group votes to see a popular, new, R-rated horror flick.

3. You are grounded, but your parents are out for the evening. Some classmates drop by and urge you to come with them "for just a few minutes."

4. In a classroom discussion about sex, the instructor says, "Raise your hands, everyone who thinks it's wrong to have sex before marriage."

5. Everyone is standing around making fun of Chester, the class geek.

Nail It Down: See in Jeremiah 26:20-23 how obedience to God can result in death.

▼ ▼ ▼ ▼ ▼ ▼ THREE LONELINESS ▼ ▼

Sara (the girl from Day 2) is doing better. The fourth day of school she met Pam, a fellow student who also just moved into the community. Turns out Pam is a Christian and lives in a neighborhood only two miles away.

Not only are the girls in the same English and science classes, but they have been doing a lot of other things together too—attending a campus Bible study, shopping at the mall, studying at the library, and participating in a freshman class project to raise money for the homeless.

Lessons from the lonely

Look It Up: Another story (about Jesus and His friends in the Garden of Gethsemane) gives us insight into how to deal with loneliness.

"They went to a place called Gethsemane, and Jesus said to his disciples, 'Sit here while I pray.' He took Peter, James and John along with him, and he began to be deeply distressed and troubled. 'My soul is overwhelmed with sorrow to the point of death,' he said to them. 'Stay here and keep watch' " (Mark 14:32-34).

Notice that Jesus relied on His human friends, but His ultimate trust was in God.

Think It Through: Writing about loneliness, Joyce Huggett notes the importance of understanding how much God loves you: "If you know yourself deeply loved by someone who will never let you down, fail you, or phase out of your life, you are rich in resources. This means that you do not spend your life searching for love. You have found it."

Have you found God's love? Have you embraced Christ?

Work It Out: If you're lonely:
1. Ask Jesus Christ to fill your life with His.
2. Develop your spiritual life through prayer, Bible study, and Scripture memory.
3. Form friendships with other Christians. Ignore those who are stuck-up, rude, and insensitive; reach out instead to people who are warm and loving.
4. Don't feel guilty. Loneliness is part of being human in a sinful world.

Nail It Down: Consider the uplifting truth of Psalm 139:7-12.

Pray About It:

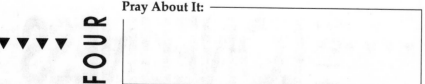

FOUR

▼ ▼ ▼ ▼

For about a month Ron (see story on Day 1) battled intense feelings of loneliness. Then he met Stevie.

Stevie, 12, has Down's syndrome. He lives in a state home and is probably the world's most serious football fan. Ron has been spending time with Stevie on a regular basis. Recently he arranged for Stevie to visit one of his team's practice sessions. And now he's making plans to take his young friend to a professional football game.

Guess what? Ron hasn't felt lonely recently.

Getting out by reaching out

Look It Up: Loneliness has been defined as the "painful awareness that we lack meaningful contact with others." So the solution is to establish some meaningful contact!

"And do not forget to do good and to share with others, for with such sacrifices God is pleased" (Hebrews 13:16).

"In everything I did, I showed you that by this kind of hard work we must help the weak, remembering the words the Lord Jesus himself said: 'It is more blessed to give than to receive' " (Acts 20:35).

Think It Through: Another good insight from Joyce Huggett: "Love is not dissipated when it is given away. It is replenished. If you want to find your way out of the maze of loneliness, therefore, you must give love."

What people in your life could use a little bit of your love today?

Work It Out: Reaching out is one of the best ways to get out of the trap of loneliness. Try these ideas:
1. Hug a family member who looks sad.
2. Write a letter to your parents and say, "I love you!"
3. Send a care package to an overseas missionary that your church supports.
4. Volunteer some time to a charitable organization or downtown mission.
5. Visit a retirement community and listen to some of the residents.
6. Organize a series of games for the little kids in your neighborhood.

Nail It Down: Read Romans 12:13-16. On Saturday, consider King David's lonely cry in Psalm 142. On Sunday, reflect on the message of Galatians 6:9-10.

▼▼▼▼▼▼ FIVE LONELINESS ▼

PARENTS
Making peace with Mom & Dad

I THINK IT'S TIME FOR A FAMILY TRUCE!

Our attitudes toward our parents are always changing.

We begin life with adoration ("My daddy can run faster than your daddy") and quickly move to teenage frustration ("You think your old man's a dweeb? You ought to see my mom!") It's only later in life that we come full circle, back to veneration ("I want you to know that I miss you, Mom . . . and I love you.")

Hopefully the next few pages will help you survive the tough time in the middle.

"Parents are the pride of their children" (Proverbs 17:6).

After last week Jeremy would like to strangle his mom.

On Monday, she wrongly blamed him for getting mud on the new carpet.

On Tuesday and Wednesday, she lectured him about his study habits.

On Thursday, she nagged him about getting a haircut.

On Friday, she criticized his friends.

The whole weekend, she grilled him about his plans.

Jeremy can hardly wait to see what next week holds!

When parents hassle you

Look It Up: Perhaps the most famous Bible verse for dealing with parents is this one:

"Children, obey your parents in the Lord, for this is right. 'Honor your father and mother'—which is the first commandment with a promise—'that it may go well with you and that you may enjoy long life on the earth' " (Ephesians 6:1-3).

Even when your parents hassle you, even when they nag, even when they act geeky, your obligation is the same—obey and show respect. Do that and Scripture says you'll be blessed.

Think It Through: Do your parents get on your nerves? Do they hassle you? If so, in what ways?

Put yourself in Jeremy's shoes. What things might he have said or done last week to make matters even worse? What sort of responses on his part might have kept the situation from getting out of hand?

Work It Out: Some helps for those horrible hassles:

1. Examine your own life. Is there truth to the things your parents are saying? Try to see things from your parents' point of view. Try to be objective.

2. Talk about the problem. Discuss your feelings openly and honestly, but make sure you are gentle and loving in tone (Ephesians 4:29-32). Nothing makes a conflict worse than a sarcastic, critical attitude.

3. Accept your parents as they are. Personality quirks just aren't worth a fight. So what if your dad dresses funny or your mom says goofy things in front of your friends? Annoying little things like that aren't worth hassling over. Instead, focus on the positive things your parents do and say.

Nail It Down: Read Proverbs 15:1 and Colossians 3:20.

ONE PARENTS

"I am so furious! Can you believe my mom's been snooping around in my room?"

"Oh yeah, I can believe it. My dad thinks he's Sherlock Holmes. He plugged the clock into the light switch the other night. When I came home after my date with Steve and cut off the lights, I didn't know it, but I also cut off the clock!"

"So?"

"So, when I said I made it home by my 11:00 p.m. curfew, my dad knew I was lying. The clock said 11:25!"

"And now you're grounded?"

"You got it."

When parents mistrust you

Look It Up: How can you get your parents to trust you?
• Be honest. "Truthful lips endure forever, but a lying tongue lasts only a moment" (Proverbs 12:19). Hey, you're not eager to trust someone who has lied to you in the past. Why should your parents be any different?
• Show maturity. "When I was a child, I talked like a child, I thought like a child, I reasoned like a child. When I became a man, I put childish ways behind me" (1 Corinthians 13:11). Question: Would you put a lot of confidence in an irresponsible little kid?
• Show respect (Deuteronomy 27:16).
In short, you gain trust by being trustworthy!

Think It Through: Do your parents trust you? Why or why not? Should they trust you?
Put it this way: If you knew your friends acted behind your back the way you act behind your parents' back, would you trust them?

Work It Out: What can you do if your mom or dad mistrusts you?
1. Humbly admit where you've been wrong. "Mom, Dad, I acted (dishonestly/immaturely/disrespectfully) when I _____ ."
2. Ask for forgiveness. "I'm sorry. I have no excuses. I was wrong. Will you please forgive me?"
3. Express your desire to change. "I don't want to be like that and I want to regain your respect. Will you tell me how I can do that?"
4. Work hard to show your sincerity. Keep your word. Don't do irresponsible things. You'll have to win back that lost trust bit by bit.

Nail It Down: A trustworthy person is refreshing—see Proverbs 25:13.

Pray About It:

TWO

Parent-child relationships can produce a lot of pain.

Larry's stepdad is verbally abusive. The cruel remarks do a Mike Tyson number on Larry's self-image.

Audrey's mom is physically abusive. She slaps five-foot, one-inch Audrey all over the house. Last spring Audrey wore sunglasses for two weeks to hide a black eye.

Shelly's dad is sexually abusive. He's been molesting Shelly for two years now.

Darren's parents are emotionally abusive. They constantly buy him stuff, but they never get involved in his life.

When parents hurt you

Look It Up: Question: What can you do when an earthly parent hurts you? Answer: Remember the love of your heavenly Father.
* He sees. "The eyes of the LORD are everywhere, keeping watch on the wicked and the good" (Proverbs 15:3).
* He cares (1 Peter 5:7).
* He comforts (Psalm 86:17).
* He heals. "He heals the brokenhearted and binds up their wounds" (Psalm 147:3).
* He promises justice. "The LORD works righteousness and justice for all the oppressed" (Psalm 103:6).

Think It Through: Parents can also hurt their children by deserting them. Few things are as painful as being abandoned, or watching your parents separate and divorce, or having a parent commit suicide. It's even common to feel rejected when a parent dies.

Can you relate to any of those situations? Do you have friends who are experiencing similar pain?

Work It Out: If you are hurting because of parental abuse (no matter what kind), seek some help—today. Call your youth leader, or make an appointment with your favorite teacher or a Christian counselor. You don't have to continue to live with all that hurt. You can find hope and healing . . . beginning with a simple phone call.

If you have friends who are the victims of parental abuse, be supportive and loving. Offer to go with them to get help. (And pray as you've never prayed before!)

Nail It Down: Reflect on God's care for His people as demonstrated in Exodus 2:23–3:4.

THREE **PARENTS**

When it comes to parents, Stuart and Matt Trumbull have a lot for which to be thankful. Their folks are happily married. Mr. and Mrs. Trumbull are also very thoughtful.

• About once a week—just as the boys get home from school— Mrs. Trumbull serves up a freshly baked dessert.

• Mr. Trumbull recently turned down a promotion because it involved a transfer that would uproot the boys.

• The Trumbulls surprised their two sons last month with a week-long camping trip to the mountains.

When parents love you

Look It Up: In a world where so many families are in trouble, it's a delight to find moms and dads who take these Bible verses seriously:

"Fathers, do not exasperate your children; instead, bring them up in the training and instruction of the Lord" (Ephesians 6:4).

"A wife of noble character who can find? She is worth far more than rubies. . . . She provides food for her family. . . . She watches over the affairs of her household" (Proverbs 31:10, 15, 27).

Hey, if you have parents like that (a gentle dad, a generous mom), you are incredibly blessed!

Think It Through: Last week Mrs. Trumbull and Matt got into a huge argument. When Mrs. Trumbull wouldn't let Matt go to a certain party, Matt accused his mom of being too strict.

Later Mrs. Trumbull realized she was being somewhat overprotective. And Matt realized his mother only expressed concern because she loved him.

Do you think most teens would rather have parents like the Trumbulls or parents who don't give a rip?

Work It Out: Maybe your parents haven't done all the things for you that the Trumbulls have done for their kids, but consider the sacrifices your folks have made. See if you can list ten specific ways your parents have demonstrated their love for you.

Now take five minutes to express your appreciation. Leave a note or give a hug or make a phone call or just say a simple "thank you"—but do something to show your gratitude!

Nail It Down: See how to respond to a loving mom (or dad for that matter)—Proverbs 31:28-29.

Pray About It:

*** *** *** FOUR

Sally's parents divorced a few months ago. Since then, the 15-year-old, soon-to-be sophomore, has been through the wringer.

Her mom cries all the time and seems barely able to function. Her dad keeps calling and asking Sally silly questions like, "Sweetie, do you still love me?" and "Honey, can you come show me how to iron a shirt?"

Sally feels pulled in two directions. How strange! Her parents are suddenly like two helpless little kids!

When parents need you

Look It Up: Believe it or not, but moms and dads need their teenage children. Not just parents with shaky marriages, but even those in strong relationships.

Can you really make a difference and be a help? Absolutely!

You can pray. "Pray in the Spirit on all occasions with all kinds of prayers and requests. With this in mind, be alert and always keep on praying for all the saints" (Ephesians 6:18).

You can listen. "My dear brothers, take note of this: Everyone should be quick to listen, slow to speak and slow to become angry" (James 1:19).

You can help. "Carry each other's burdens, and in this way you will fulfill the law of Christ" (Galatians 6:2).

Think It Through: Are your parents facing:
- Unexpected pressures at work or loss of a job?
- Health problems?
- The illness or loss of their own parents?
- Added responsibilities at church or at home?
- Depression or other emotional difficulties?

Work It Out: Here are some ideas for those times when your parents need you:
1. Do a task your dad hates.
2. Run an errand for your mom.
3. Volunteer to clear the table and do the dishes.
4. Offer to fix dinner.
5. Say, "I love you."
6. Give a hug and/or kiss.
7. Leave an encouraging note where they'll see it.
8. Do the laundry.

Nail It Down: Read Proverbs 23:22. On Saturday consider Leviticus 19:3. On Sunday reflect on Proverbs 6:20-23.

FIVE PARENTS

PEER PRESSURE * * *
Who controls your life?

A t its worst, peer pressure is like a giant vacuum cleaner that hovers (or should we say "hoovers"?) above your head, clicking on at the worst possible moments. You're minding your own business, and VAROOM! Suddenly there's this incredible force tugging at you. If you weaken for even a split second . . . WHOOSH! Away you go, and where you end up is anybody's guess. Want some ideas on how to resist the pull of the crowd?

"Do not conform any longer to the pattern of this world" (Romans 12:2).

Matt attended a small Christian school from kindergarten through 8th grade. This year he made the transition to a very large public high school. It's been a whole new world for Matt. It's also been a time of inner turmoil.

Friday night Matt went out with some guys at his new school. About nine o'clock, someone said, "Hey, let's cruise into the city."

Matt thought to himself, "That's 70 miles away! I'm supposed to be home by 11:00." But he didn't say a word. And he didn't get home until after 1:00 a.m.!

"I just want to fit in"

Look It Up: Peer pressure is the emotional force friends apply to try to get us to do (or not do) certain things. It's an old phenomenon; in fact, Solomon warned his sons about it long ago.

"My son, if sinners entice you, do not give in to them. If they say, 'Come along with us . . . throw in your lot with us, and we will share a common purse'—my son, do not go along with them, do not set foot on their paths; for their feet rush into sin, they are swift to shed blood. . . These men lie in wait for their own blood; they waylay only themselves!" (Proverbs 1:10-11, 14-16, 18).

Think It Through: Why do you think peer pressure is so intense? Where does peer pressure hit you the hardest? If you found yourself in a situation like the one Matt faced, how do you think you would respond?

Work It Out: Begin your study of peer pressure with this prayer:

"Father, I need wisdom to both understand and learn to deal with peer pressure. Give me an open heart to hear what You want to say to me. And cause me to have a willing spirit, so that I might put into practice the things I learn. In Jesus' name I pray. Amen."

Then do this experiment: Today at school, watch for examples of peer pressure in action. Observe how your classmates are affected. See if you can isolate and identify some of the techniques people use to pressure each other.

Nail It Down: Read the warning in Proverbs 28:10—especially if you're applying negative peer pressure to others.

********* **ONE** **PEER PRESSURE**

A fter his week-
end adven-
ture (see Day 1),
Matt was threat-
ened with almost
every form of pun-
ishment known to
humankind. Now
three days into a
judgment of "three
weeks with no
privileges," Matt is
pretty sure he'll
speak up next time
the gang suggests a
night on the town.
"I was pretty
stupid," he admits.

Meanwhile,
Matt's best
Christian friend
Michael is liking
the party scene
more and more.

Be strong and guard your faith!

Look It Up: First, negative peer pressure prompts poor decisions.

"Wanting to release Jesus, Pilate appealed to them again. But they kept shouting, 'Crucify him! Crucify him!'

"For the third time he spoke to them: 'Why? . . . I have found in him no grounds for the death penalty. Therefore I will have him punished and then release him.'

"But with loud shouts they insistently demanded that he be crucified, and their shouts prevailed. So Pilate decided to grant their demand" (Luke 23:20-24).

Second, negative peer pressure harms one's relationship with God.

"Then the Israelites did evil in the eyes of the LORD and served the Baals. They forsook the LORD, the God of their fathers . . . They followed and worshiped various gods of the peoples around them. They provoked the LORD to anger" (Judges 2:11-12).

Think It Through: Have you let others pressure you into a bad decision this week? Are certain friends and/or activities pulling you away from God?

Work It Out: Here are some tips for saying no:

1. Mark out firmly in your own mind what you will and won't do. That way you stand a much better chance of resisting pressure.

2. Be firm. The crowd can be like a school of sharks. If they sense any hesitation, they'll go for the kill.

3. Let people know that though you like them, you can't participate in certain activities.

Nail It Down: See how peer pressure can damage your faith—Numbers 25:1-2.

Pray About It:

✱✱✱✱✱✱ T W O

His three week grounding is behind him. And Matt is determined not to get in major trouble like that again.

Yesterday, he ate lunch with Peggy, a girl from his youth group. She told him about "Prime Time."

"What's that?"

"It's like a Bible study before school every Tuesday. This guy named Greg leads it. A lot of juniors go. And a few freshmen. Plus, every winter break Greg and his wife take a bunch of kids skiing."

"Is it any good?"

"I think it's really good!"

Finding a few faithful friends

Look It Up: Peggy is smart to seek out some Christian friends. Why?

1. If you hang around with non-Christians all the time, you may eventually yield to their negative influence.

"Do not set foot on the path of the wicked or walk in the way of evil men" (Proverbs 4:14).

"Do not envy wicked men, do not desire their company" (Proverbs 24:1).

2. On the other hand, Christian peers can surround you with positive peer pressure. "He who walks with the wise grows wise, but a companion of fools suffers harm" (Proverbs 13:20).

Think It Through: Earlier we compared negative peer pressure to a huge, floating vacuum cleaner that sucks up weak individuals. Today, you need to realize that positive peer pressure is like a surge of mega-gravity! In stormy times, positive influences can keep you standing strong . . . right where you need to be!

Work It Out: What can you do to find some committed Christian friends?

• Become more involved in your church's youth group and Sunday school programs.

• Attend the meetings of various campus ministry groups— Fellowship of Christian Athletes, Student Venture, Campus Life, Young Life, and others.

• Try to get permission to start a before-school or after-school Bible study. With approval, pass out some flyers and tape up a few posters. You might be surprised at what happens. A bunch of new Christian friends? A chance to minister to an interested non-Christian or two? Go for it!

Nail It Down: Read 1 Corinthians 15:33-34.

******* THREE **PEER PRESSURE**

At a party after the first football game, Ted is the center of attention. He intercepted a pass in the last minute to secure a 14-10 victory. All the guys are slapping him on the back. All the girls are telling him how wonderful he is.

Suddenly, someone pops the top on a can of beer and says, "Hey, Ted! For all you do, this brew's for you!" Everyone is laughing and watching.

After a long pause, Ted says, "Thanks, but I think I'll just have some pop."

Daring to be different!

Look It Up: Gutsy people dare to be different. Two examples:

1. Most of the Israelite spies who cased out the Promised Land considered conquering it to be a lost cause. "The people who live there are powerful, and the cities are fortified and very large. We even saw descendants of Anak there" (Numbers 13:28).

Enter Caleb—a guy who refused to bow to peer pressure. Opposing the majority, he said, "We should go up and take possession of the land, for we can certainly do it" (Numbers 13:30).

2. When the king of Jericho put serious pressure on Rahab, she stuck with the Israelites. "The LORD your God is God in heaven above and on the earth below. Now then, please swear to me by the LORD that you will show kindness to my family, because I have shown kindness to you" (Joshua 2:11-12).

Think It Through: Caleb and Rahab stood up against the crowd. Do you?

What do you think about Ted's response? How would you have reacted in his situation?

Work It Out: Do something today to express your independence and unique personality.

• Dress a little bit differently from the others in your group.

• Don't use the popular word or phrase that other people at your school are saying every two minutes.

• Develop an unusual interest like mime, or art history, or puppetry. (Hey, you can't stand up on big issues until you first do it in small ways.)

Nail It Down: Read in Daniel 3 about three teenagers who stood strong in the face of *extreme* pressure.

Pray About It:

✳✳✳✳✳✳ FOUR

After two Thompson Senior High School students died in separate alcohol-related accidents, Martha decided it was time to exert a positive influence.

She first wrote a stirring editorial for the school paper. Then, with the help of her guidance counselor, she organized "Weekend Workout."

What is Weekend Workout? It's a Friday night function at Martha's church gymnasium. From nine until midnight each week, teens play volleyball, basketball, and participate in aerobics classes.

Everyone just loves it!

You can steer your peers

Look It Up: Can one person really affect a whole group? Is it possible to steer your peers in the right direction . . . when they're going the wrong way? Yes!

"You are the light of the world. A city on a hill cannot be hidden. Neither do people light a lamp and put it under a bowl. Instead they put it on its stand, and it gives light to everyone in the house. In the same way, let your light shine before men, that they may see your good deeds and praise your Father in heaven" (Matthew 5:14-16).

Think It Through: List the problems and predicaments that your friends most often fall into. Now list some ways you could steer your peers away from those troublesome situations.

When the time comes this weekend, will you make the tough choice to stand up and encourage the group to do the right thing?

If you won't, who will?

Work It Out: So far, we've only scratched the surface of the widespread problem of peer pressure.

If you'd like to explore the issue in greater detail, we heartily recommend Chris Lutes's book *Peer Pressure: Making it work for you!* (Campus Life Books, Zondervan Publishing House).

You might even consider gathering some friends and studying this resource in a group setting.

Nail It Down: Check out how Gamaliel's cool-headed response altered his peer group's actions—Acts 5:29-40. On Saturday, consider the effect young King Josiah had on the nation of Judah—2 Chronicles 34 (especially verses 31-32). On Sunday, contemplate how unaffected by peer pressure the Apostle Paul was—2 Corinthians 6:3-11.

✳ ✳ ✳ ✳ ✳ ✳ ✳ FIVE **PEER PRESSURE**

THE CASE OF THE EMPTY

Almost 2,000 years ago, Jesus Christ was crucified and buried. Three days later, his grave was mysteriously empty!

Explanations. Some say that Jesus' disciples stole His body and faked His resurrection. Others argue that Jesus really didn't die—He merely fainted, revived in the tomb, and somehow escaped.

What Really Happened? The best way to know for sure what took place on that Sunday morning is to examine the written accounts. Matthew, John, and Peter were all eyewitnesses to the life, death, and resurrection of Jesus (Matthew 28; John 20; 1 Peter 1:3; and 2 Peter 1:16).

These events didn't happen in secret. They were public incidents. In fact, the Apostle Paul wrote that Jesus appeared to over 500 people after His resurrection, and that most of them were still living at the time of his writing and *could* verify the resurrection story (1 Corinthians 15:6).

No Other Explanation Fits. Jesus was dead, no doubt about it (Mark 15:44-45). Pilate, the governor of the Jews, in order to protect against Jesus' disciples stealing His body, posted a "Rambo" unit of Roman guards outside the tomb and then sealed it with his official seal (Matthew 27:63-66). Breaking such a seal was punishable by death. And yet, Jesus' body was missing on Sunday morning! Are we supposed to believe that a scared group of disciples somehow found the courage to overpower battle-hardened Roman soldiers?

And why would the disciples have committed their lives to telling others that Christ had risen if they knew that the resurrection was a hoax? History tells us that almost all of them died for the sake of Christ. Granted, people sometimes die for a lie, but not when they *know* it's a lie!

Question: What happened to cause all these individuals to give their lives telling others that Christ was alive? Answer: They must have seen the risen Savior!

Does the empty tomb really matter? Absolutely! The resurrection of Christ is so central to the gospel that Paul concludes, *"If Christ has not been raised, your faith is futile; you are still in your sins"* (1 Corinthians 15:17). Thank God for the empty tomb! Thank God that *"Christ has indeed been raised from the dead"* (1 Corinthians 15:20)!

FATHERHOOD

"**H**ey, Bill! What hit you—a Mack truck?"

"Aw, you know my dad. Sometimes I think all he wants to do is punch my lights out. He makes me wish I'd never been born."

Abusive or caring, critical or concerned, parents come in all sizes and shapes. But good or bad, *their* actions and attitudes shape your idea of what a *parent* is like. And, their parenting also gives you your first concept of what *God* is like as a Father. As a result, God can get a bum rap! Why? Because sometimes our parents blow it.

For example, Bill's whole idea of what a father is like comes from a dad who communicates displeasure, rejection, and anger. Under these circumstances, how do you think Bill might learn to respond to God, his heavenly Father? How would *you*?

Can someone like Bill, who hasn't had a great earthly father, learn to know God as the loving, heavenly Father He is? The answer is *YES*!

God did two things that make it easy to get to know Him. First, He wrote about Himself in the Bible. Second, He came to earth in human form to let us know just how much He loves us. If you want to see how God behaves and responds to people, then look at Jesus.

Jesus accepts His people as they are. Uncritically. Nonjudgmentally. Without anger. Always with love. Yet He never tolerates sin or lets it slide by. He deals with the sin and it is over. Jesus brings the best out of those He loves.

Do you want to get to know God as your Father? Then get to know Jesus. Know Him as He forgave one of His best friends, who had lied about even knowing Him. Know Him as He ate His last meal with His closest friends and washed their dirty feet while preparing to die; and as He prayed earnestly to His Father that you and He would be one in heart. Above all, know Him as He came bursting out of a tomb, *full* of life for all who truly want it.

Jesus. Through Him you can know the *perfect* Father!

APPEARANCE
Getting to the heart of the matter

No doubt about it—appearances are important in this world. A good looking guy or girl can cause heads to turn, eyes to bulge, and hearts to flutter.

But how important are appearances to God? Very important? A little important? Not important at all?

Keep reading for some important answers!

"But the LORD said to Samuel, 'Do not consider his appearance or his height, for I have rejected him. The LORD does not look at the things man looks at. Man looks at the outward appearance, but the LORD looks at the heart" (1 Samuel 16:7).

The ritual takes place every afternoon at the Osborn Swim Club. The girls eye the guys: "Ben is soooo gorgeous! Like, I could stare at him for hours."

"What do you mean you could stare. You do stare—and drool!"

Meanwhile on the other side of the pool . . . the guys scope out the girls: "I'm gonna marry somebody who looks just like Shannon."

"Shannon has the IQ of a brick."

"So what?"

Obsessed with the outside!

Look It Up: Much of our culture is obsessed with outer appearance, but Christians are commanded to focus on our inner condition.

"Your beauty should not come from outward adornment, such as braided hair and the wearing of gold jewelry and fine clothes. Instead, it should be that of your inner self, the unfading beauty of a gentle and quiet spirit, which is of great worth in God's sight" (1 Peter 3:3-4).

The apostle Paul stressed this same point when he encountered some shallow people in his day.

"As for those who seemed to be important—whatever they were makes no difference to me; God does not judge by external appearance—those men added nothing to my message" (Galatians 2:6).

Think It Through: Flashy clothes on a sculpted body in a hot car—suppose you get all that. You manage to achieve "the look" (whatever "the look" is). Suddenly everybody wants to date you or be your friend.

Where were all these people before? Why did they only come around after you changed your appearance? Do all these "new friends" like you—the real person inside—or just your image?

Work It Out: No doubt about it . . . we all want to look good. But be careful! If you get caught up in the appearance trap you'll never be satisfied. Average looks will make you jealous and bitter. Good looks will spark suspicion—even fear.

Start your study this week with an honest prayer. Tell God how you feel about your own appearance. Then ask Him to show you His point of view.

Nail It Down: Read about people who prized outer appearance above all else—2 Corinthians 5:12.

❖ ❖ ❖ ❖ ❖ ❖ ❖ ONE **APPEARANCE** ❖ ❖

Debbie B. goes to a Christian school. She also attends church and youth group faithfully.

That's not all. Debbie works in a Christian bookstore, has a regular quiet time, and listens only to Christian music. Moreover, she has vowed to date only Christian guys.

If outer conduct was all that mattered to God, Debbie would have it made in the shade. No one acts more religious.

But God—as we saw yesterday—cares most about a person's inner condition. And Debbie's heart is full of pride, jealousy, and selfishness.

Appearances can be deceiving!

Look It Up: Do you recall the harsh words Jesus spoke to the religious people of His day?

"Woe to you, teachers of the law and Pharisees, you hypocrites! You clean the outside of the cup and dish, but inside they are full of greed and self-indulgence. Blind Pharisee! First clean the inside of the cup and dish, and then the outside also will be clean.

"Woe to you, teachers of the law and Pharisees, you hypocrites! You are like whitewashed tombs, which look beautiful on the outside but on the inside are full of dead men's bones and everything unclean. In the same way, on the outside you appear to people as righteous but on the inside you are full of hypocrisy and wickedness" (Matthew 23:27-28).

Think It Through: Based on what Jesus told the Pharisees, is a person who is doing right things automatically right with God?

Are you living like a Pharisee?

Work It Out: Evaluate your own spiritual conduct. Are you mechanically "going through the motions"? Is your primary motive "to be seen by others and to be thought of as a neat person"? If so:

• Confess your wrong attitudes (1 John 1:9).
• Return to your first love (Revelation 2:4). Make Jesus—not appearances—your top priority.
• Quit seeking the praise of men (John 12:43).
• Make a renewed effort to practice Christianity in secret as well as in public (Matthew 6:1-8).

Nail It Down: Have you read about the "Pharisaical" people in Colossae who had their focus in the wrong place? See Colossians 2:20-23.

Pray About It:

❖ ❖ ❖ ❖ ❖

T W O

The following are three very questionable situations:

1. Sixteen-year-old Randy is seen hanging out in front of a local liquor store.

2. Carol and her boyfriend Taylor, both sophomores at college, are taking a weekend trip with another couple to a nearby resort. The two guys and two girls are staying in the same motel room.

3. Kyle is seen giving money to Billy S. on the same day that everyone knows Billy's been selling copies of Mrs. Schenk's English test.

Appearing to be bad?

Look It Up: One of the recurring themes of the New Testament is that a Christian must be extremely careful to avoid the appearance of wrongdoing and to strive for a good reputation.

• "But among you there must not be even a hint of sexual immorality, or of any kind of impurity, or of greed, because these are improper for God's holy people" (Ephesians 5:3).

• "Avoid every kind of evil" (1 Thessalonians 5:22).

• "He must also have a good reputation with outsiders, so that he will not fall into disgrace and into the devil's trap" (1 Timothy 3:7).

Think It Through: Going back to the examples cited, what behaviors do those situations suggest?

Do we know that Randy is buying booze? Or that Carol and Taylor are having sex? Or that Kyle is purchasing a hot test? Maybe not. But at the same time their behavior does raise serious questions.

Work It Out: Sit down with a close Christian friend and discuss the stories of Randy, Carol and Taylor, and Kyle. Assume that in each of the situations nothing sinful is taking place. Now, can you come up with a better plan in each case?

Take a few moments to examine your own lives. Are you making ambiguous remarks or doing questionable things? Determine to be careful about every activity that might be misunderstood.

Hold each other accountable in the days ahead. A little carelessness can cause a lot of heartache!

Nail It Down: Check out Nehemiah's concern with living in such a way that God's name would not be dragged through the mud—Nehemiah 5:1-11.

✦✦✦✦✦✦✦✦✦ THREE **APPEARANCE** ✦✦

Back to Randy (the guy from yesterday's story).

What we didn't tell you before is that Randy just became a Christian a few weeks ago. Faith in Christ is totally new to him.

On the one hand, Randy has made some big changes. But on the other hand, he still has some glaring faults—like his fighting, his cursing, and his lack of control over his thoughts.

The ultimate disappearing act

Look It Up: All this week we've been stressing the need to be careful about how things appear. Today we want to emphasize the things that need to disappear!

"Put to death, therefore, whatever belongs to your earthly nature: sexual immorality, impurity, lust, evil desires and greed, which is idolatry. Because of these, the wrath of God is coming. You used to walk in these ways, in the life you once lived. But now you must rid yourselves of all such things as these: anger, rage, malice, slander, and filthy language from your lips. Do not lie to each other, since you have taken off your old self with its practices and have put on the new self, which is being renewed in knowledge in the image of its Creator" (Colossians 3:5-10).

Think It Through: If Randy was your friend, how would you try to help him?

Is growth something we must wait for God to do? What does Colossians 3:5-10 say?

Work It Out: Check whether the behaviors and/or attitudes described above are present in your life:

	YES	NO
1. Sexual immorality	___	___
2. Lust	___	___
3. Evil desires	___	___
4. Greed	___	___
5. Anger/Rage	___	___
6. Filthy language	___	___
7. Lying	___	___

Write this on an index card: "You must rid yourself of ____ ." Fill in the blank with the above items you checked yes. Memorize it . . . and do what it says.

Nail It Down: Read more about evil in Psalm 24:3-4.

Pray About It:

FOUR

❖ ❖ ❖ ❖ ❖ ❖

Your favorite teacher says, "Teens are having sex. And teens are having babies. Obviously, birth control should be more readily available."

Your favorite TV star says, "It's outrageous that a few right-wing religious extremists are trying to control what's on TV! Let them just turn their sets off. Let the rest of us watch what we want!"

Your least favorite class-mate screams, "If abortion is outlawed, women will die because of back-alley abortions!"

Getting beneath the surface

Look It Up: Many people don't think critically. If a statement seems right, they just accept it. But Jesus calls Christians to dig deeper. "Stop judging by mere appearances, and make a right judgment" (John 7:24).

Think It Through: The statements at the beginning of this page seem sensible. But underneath each one lies an assumption that's not so sensible.

1. Your teacher assumes that birth control lessens the number of teen pregnancies. Wrong! Planned Parenthood's own 1986 study shows the following:

• The more that birth control is available to teens, the more they have sex . . . and get pregnant.

• The only two factors that effectively lessen the number of teen pregnancies are frequent church attendance and parental guidance.

2. The TV star assumes that watching pornography is harmless. But studies show that pornography is directly linked with an increase in violent sex crimes like rape and child molestation.

3. Your classmate assumes that we should take more pity on the mother than on the baby she is trying to kill.

Work It Out: Learn to get beneath the surface of ideas. Ask tough questions about the meaning of a popular song, the message of a new movie, the claims of a dynamic speaker. Don't judge them "by mere appearances." Instead, with the Bible as your guide, discern carefully.

Nail It Down: See how Jesus got beneath the surface (John 3:1-21). On Saturday, read Proverbs 26:4. Ask God to remove any foolish ideas or beliefs you might have. On Sunday, read Proverbs 26:5. Are you willing to be used by God in exposing the assumptions of those who are wise in their own eyes?

❖ ❖ ❖ ❖ ❖ ❖ ❖ FIVE APPEARANCE ❖ ❖

· · INTOLERANCE · · ·
The hostilities must cease!

Jesus raised a ruckus when he said, "Love your neighbors—all your neighbors."

People simply couldn't (perhaps, wouldn't is a better word) deal with that requirement. After 2,000 years, most still won't face up to it.

"You mean love everyone?"

"Yes."

"Even people you don't really like?"

"Especially those you don't really like."

"But that's not natural!"

"That's right! It's supernatural!"

"For he himself [Christ] is our peace, who has made the two one and has destroyed the barrier, the dividing wall of hostility" (Ephesians 2:14).

Lewis and Leonard laugh about their first meeting.

Lewis: "I thought he was a dumb jock. I didn't want to have anything to do with him!"

Leonard: "I remember thinking, 'Oh, great! I'm going to be living next door to a freak!' His hair was kind of long, and he had—shall we say—different musical tastes."

It's a good thing the guys didn't stick with their first impressions. Over the last year they have become extremely close friends.

Labels: Easy . . . and wrong!

Look It Up: We are masters at labeling. We see someone. We quickly examine his or her appearance and/or behavior. We make a snap judgment, assign a label, and then—if it's a category that's threatening or different—we dismiss the person. How easy . . . how convenient . . . how wrong!

Such intolerance almost kept Nathanael from meeting Christ!

"Philip found Nathanael and told him, 'We have found the one Moses wrote about in the Law, and about whom the prophets also wrote—Jesus of Nazareth, the son of Joseph.'

" 'Nazareth! Can anything good come from there?' Nathanael asked.

" 'Come and see, ' said Philip" (John 1:45-46).

Fortunately, Nathanael went beyond labeling. Because he did, he found a friend—and a Savior (1:49)—in Jesus Christ.

Think It Through: The world says, "First impressions are everything!" Christ says that we must get beyond the surface (1 Samuel 16:7) in order to appreciate the uniqueness of each individual.

Are you missing out on a potentially great friendship because you have wrongly labeled someone?

Work It Out: List the categories you use to label people at your school and in your church. What labels do you think people attach to you? Read Galatians 3:26-28. What does this passage indicate about labeling others?

Reach out today to someone in a different category. Look beyond the surface fact that he or she is a freak, a jock, a brain, a geek, etc. Try to get to know the real person behind the label.

Nail It Down: See an instance in which labeling had devastating consequences—Mark 6:1-6.

ONE INTOLERANCE

Angie is the self-appointed judge of Quinnsworth Academy.

Some of her recent "court" decisions:

• "I don't see how a good Christian could possibly go into a restaurant that serves alcohol."

• "I went to that church once. Let me tell you—those people are weird!"

• "As far as I'm concerned, anybody who would waste their time listening to that kind of music, is headed for big trouble."

Have gavel, will travel

Look It Up: Wielding their invisible gavels, many Christians like to make judgments on all the wrong things they think they see others doing.

The Bible warns against such intolerant behavior:

"There is only one Lawgiver and Judge, the one who is able to save and destroy. But you—who are you to judge your neighbor?" (James 4:12).

"Therefore let us stop passing judgment on one another" (Romans 14:13).

We're experts at finding fault with others. We fail when it comes to accepting others (Romans 15:7).

Think It Through: Judging others is often pride in disguise. We see someone whose behavior may not be wrong, but he or she is doing something we wouldn't do. With one carefully phrased sentence, we not only rip up that person, we also try to build up ourselves!

Example: "I really wonder about him . . . he's missed youth group three times in a row." Translation: "I don't wonder about me. I've been to group every week. I'm so good!"

Work It Out: Stop being judgmental! Every time you find yourself questioning the motives of others:

1. Remember that only God knows the motives of an individual's heart (1 Corinthians 4:5).

2. Remember that you will stand before Christ one day (Romans 14:10).

3. Quit focusing on others and concentrate on your own responsibilities before God (John 21:18-22).

A good rule of thumb: On issues where God's Word is clear, there is no debate; however, in life's gray areas we must be tolerant, allowing others to be convicted under the direction of the Holy Spirit.

Nail It Down: Read Matthew 7:1-5.

Pray About It:

TWO

Raymond Davis, 15, is a committed Christian, a good student, and a top-notch baseball player. He is friendly and fun to be around. He is also black.

A month ago the Davis family moved into an all-white neighborhood. Since that time, their dog has been poisoned and racial slurs have been spray-painted on their garage doors.

Last night, someone demolished their mailbox.

"I don't get it," Raymond whispers. "What did we ever do to deserve this?"

The poison of prejudice

Look It Up: What is wrong with prejudice? Plenty!

• It fails to take into account that all people have dignity and value, because we are all created in the image of God (Genesis 1:26-28).

• It forgets that, in a general sense, we're all ultimately related (Genesis 5:3-5; Acts 17:26).

• It stems from pride, is based on hatred, and is fueled by fear. (Esther 3:1-6; John 4:4-9).

• It ignores the fact that God's family will ultimately include people from every race and culture. "After this I looked and there before me was a great multitude that no one could count, from every nation, tribe, people and language, standing before the throne and in front of the Lamb" (Revelation 7:9).

Think It Through: Imagine having car trouble on the interstate. Soon a car pulls over. The driver is a big guy of a different racial background from yours. He walks toward you. What is going through your mind?

What if that person was your same color? Would you feel more comfortable? What does that say about you?

Since God seems to be colorblind, why are we so obsessed with the tint of a person's skin?

Work It Out: If you are the victim of prejudice, take comfort in the fact the Jesus knows how you feel. He too was rejected, the object of frequent name calling (John 1:46; 10:19-20; Mark 6:1-6).

If you think you might have a problem with prejudice (whether racial or otherwise), pray: "Lord, change my heart. Give me a love for everyone—especially for those who are different from me. Amen."

Nail It Down: Read about economic prejudice—James 2:1-4.

■ ■ ■ ■ ■ ■ ■ **THREE INTOLERANCE**

As Larry and his sister drive past the Davis house (see the story on Day 3), he starts fuming.

"Okay, I know I probably have some prejudice, but I would never do anything like that! These are supposed to be civilized people in this neighborhood. This is supposed to be the 20th century! Who cares if the Davises are black?"

Pam just shakes her head, "Obviously some people care a lot."

"Well it makes me feel embarrassed to know that I'm even partly prejudiced."

Pam shrugs, "Me too. So how do we change?"

Bye-bye to bigotry

Look It Up: Never fear, Pam and Larry. God's Word has lots of ideas about how to respond to prejudice.

1. We must look to Christ. Only He can tear down the barriers that separate individuals and races (Ephesians 2:11-12).

2. We must be willing to befriend those who are different. (In Acts 9:43 we read about Peter, a Jew, staying with a man who tanned skins for a living. Most Jews would not have gone near a person who worked with animal carcasses and hides, much less, stayed in his house!)

3. We must be able to say as Peter did, "I now realize how true it is that God does not show favoritism but accepts men from every nation who fear him and do what is right" (Acts 10:34-35).

4. We must stand up against those who are intolerant (Galatians 2:11-14).

Think It Through: If you had a friend of a different race who was being persecuted, how would you react?

What do you think Jesus Christ thinks about those individuals who are trying to run the Davises out of their neighborhood?

What is the most prejudicial act you've ever committed? Why do you think you did it?

Work It Out: Here are some practical ways to overcome bigotry:
- Ask God to help you change your attitudes.
- Eat lunch with someone from a different race.
- Visit an ethnic church.
- Read a magazine that expresses a different racial or cultural viewpoint.

Nail It Down: Read about how God shattered religious prejudice in Acts 11:1-18.

Pray About It:

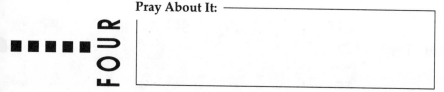

FOUR

145

Guess what? After nearly three months had passed, the police arrested three men and charged them with spray-painting the racial slurs on the Davises' garage. The youngest of the suspects eventually signed a confession admitting everything—even poisoning the Davises' dog.

But then an amazing thing happened. Mr. Davis refused to press charges.

"That's not necessary. Those men had my forgiveness long ago. I just want to live in peace here with my family. Please, that's all I want."

Be merciful— not merciless!

Look It Up: Mr. Davis is unusual. Most people in his situation would be screaming for justice. But the Bible gently reminds us of a more tolerant way.

1. Our heavenly Father is merciful (Micah 7:18).

2. We are to be like our heavenly Father. "Be imitators of God, therefore, as dearly loved children" (Ephesians 5:1).

3. Therefore, we must be merciful to others. "Be merciful, just as your Father is merciful" (Luke 6:36).

Think It Through: Mercy means loving and accepting others even when they don't deserve it. It means choosing to overlook their shortcomings and differences.

One can't be prejudiced or bigoted, and also be merciful. Like oil and water, intolerance and mercy simply do not mix.

Are you a merciful person? Could you have done what Mr. Davis did? Would you have done that?

If God suddenly refused to deal with us mercifully, where would we be?

Work It Out: Practice mercy today.

• Forgive that family member who recently hurt your feelings.

• Resist the urge to strike back at that classmate who has it in for you.

• Refuse to answer back when someone speaks ill of you.

• Show compassion to someone who is trapped in sin. Don't shun such people! On the contrary, let them see the love of Christ.

Nail It Down: Read Matthew 5:7 today. On Saturday, check out an instance when the Apostle Paul was wrongly labeled—Acts 28:1-6. Then on Sunday, think about the implications of Luke 6:27-35.

FIVE INTOLERANCE

*S*cenario No. 1: An employer refuses to hire James simply because he is black. Is that *racism?*

Scenario No. 2: A different employer refuses to hire Stuart simply because he is white. Is that *racism?*

Scenario No. 3: A high court rules that preferential treatment in hiring practices must be given to one racial group over another. Is that *racism?*

What is Racism? Simply put, racism is any form of prejudice (prejudging) based solely on race. If you act toward a person in a certain way simply because he or she belongs to a different race, you're guilty of racism.

The Root of Racism. Most of us gravitate toward others with whom we have much in common. There's nothing necessarily wrong with that.

Two people of different races *look* different. What's more, since different races sometimes have different cultural and social traditions, two people from different races may *think* and/or *act* differently in certain situations. These differences can make people uncomfortable with each other. There's nothing necessarily wrong with that either.

Racism happens when we let those differences (both real and imagined) unjustifiably divide us. Racism says, "Since that person is different, he (or she) must be inferior. I, and the rest of my kind, deserve better treatment." Is that a Biblical attitude?

The Bible and Racism. All people are created in the image of God (Genesis 1:26-27); therefore we should treat each person God brings into our lives with respect and dignity—regardless of race.

Jesus demonstrated this truth for us. He reached out in love to a Samaritan woman during a time when other Jews hated the inhabitants of Samaria. (They were despised because of their mixed descent.) Our Lord showed that differences—whether ethnic, cultural, or racial—should not foster racism.

Let's follow the example of Christ even as we remember this great pronouncement: *"You are all sons of God through faith in Christ Jesus. . . . There is neither Jew nor Greek, slave nor free, male nor female, for you are all one in Christ Jesus" (Galatians 3:26, 28).*

THE **BIGGEST** EVENTS
IN THE HISTORY OF THE WORLD

Creation

Adam & Eve sin
in the Garden of Eden

Invention
of the wheel

Moses receives the
Ten Commandments
at Mount Sinai

Birth of
Jesus Christ

Death, burial,
& resurrection
of Jesus Christ

The Middle Ages

World War II

The Berlin Wall
tumbles down

A reader of this
page believes in
Jesus Christ &
finds eternal life

The Second Coming
of Jesus Christ

New heaven
& new earth

There have been some huge happenings in the history of this old
earth—far too many to list on this page. And some of the biggest
events are yet to come . . . like maybe your own salvation.

Have you ever asked Christ to forgive your sins and be your Savior?
If not, do it right now—today.

Go ahead, make some history.

WORLD RELIGIONS
How many ways to God?

The human race is incredibly religious.

No matter where you go, belief in a Supreme Being is the rule, not the exception. In every culture, we observe men and women striving to understand, know, and serve their Creator.

But there are great differences too—conflicting religious systems that raise troubling questions.

Who's right? Who's wrong? Are there many ways to God? And does it really matter?

"Salvation is found in no one else, for there is no other name under heaven given to men by which we must be saved" (Acts 4:12).

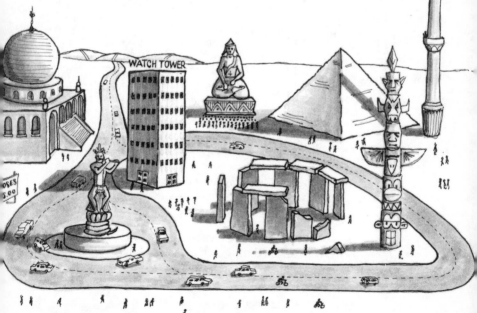

Last night on TV there was a special report on the events taking place in the Arab world. The reporter kept referring to the "Islamic revolution."

Today Connie and her little sister Kim see a Muslim woman on the bus. She's wearing a veil over her face and head.

Pointing, Kim blurts, "Look at that funny lady!"

"Kim! Don't point!" mumbles Connie, an embarrassed look on her face.

The explosive world of Islam!

Look It Up: The Islamic holy book, called the Qur'an (or Koran), teaches some concepts that Christians also believe—the existence of a good, all-powerful God (they call him *Allah*); the reality of angels and demons; and the doctrine of a final judgment.

However, Muslims regard Jesus as a mere prophet —on the same level with Abraham, Moses, and Muhammad. They claim Christ never died (death is a sign of failure, and prophets do not fail). Moreover, Muslims deny that Jesus was God in the flesh.

Yet the Bible clearly claims that Jesus is God.

"About the Son [God] says, 'Your throne, O God, will last forever and ever' " (Hebrews 1:8).

"In the beginning was the Word, and the Word was with God, and the Word was God" (John 1:1).

Think It Through: Fast facts on Islam—
• The term *Islam* is derived from an Arabic word which means "commitment" or "surrender."
• Islam traces its roots to Muhammad who was born in Mecca, Arabia, about A.D. 571.
• Islam claims well over half a billion followers worldwide. That number is rapidly rising each year!
• Devout Muslims (followers of Islam) are very moral. They pray five times daily; give regularly to charity; and condemn adultery, divorce, and usury.
• Just as Christianity has various denominations, so Islam also has different groups. The two primary factions are the Sunni Muslims and the Shi'ite Muslims.

Work It Out: Pray for those missionaries working among Muslim peoples—for their safety and endurance and for open hearts among those who hear the gospel.

Nail It Down: Notice that the soldiers at the crucifixion certified the death of Jesus—John 19:31-34.

∞ ∞ ∞ ∞ ∞ ∞ ∞ ∞ ∞ **ONE WORLD RELIGIONS** ∘

K ate is shocked as she watches a film about India in her geography class.

She sees cattle roaming freely through the busy streets of Calcutta. She stares at people who are drinking and bathing in the dirty waters of the Ganges River. She watches footage of gurus being worshiped and of poor people being ignored on the streets.

"I don't understand. Why do they live like that?"

The answer is Hinduism.

When karmas run over dogmas

Look It Up: In addition to their one High God (called Brahman, "the Absolute"), Hindus also believe in as many as 330 million lesser gods. Yet the Bible states, "This is what the LORD says—Israel's King and Redeemer, the LORD Almighty: I am the first and I am the last; apart from me there is no God" (Isaiah 44:6).

Furthermore, Hinduism teaches three ways of salvation: knowledge, works of religious observance, and devotion to the gods.

This contradicts Christian teaching that salvation is a gift of God that we can receive but never earn.

"He saved us, not because of righteous things we had done, but because of his mercy. He saved us through the washing of rebirth and renewal by the Holy Spirit" (Titus 3:5).

Think It Through: Did you know the following?
• Hinduism began more than 3,000 years ago.
• The Hindu scriptures are called the *Vedas*.
• There are about 500 million Hindus in the world.
• Yoga is the spiritual discipline used by Hindus to help them join their soul (called *atman*) with the world soul (*paramatman*).
• *Karma* is the word used to describe the universal law of cause and effect. For example, bad karma means punishment for misdeeds in a previous life or reincarnation.

Work It Out: Is anyone you know involved in yoga? Hey, it's not just neutral exercising. Read up on the topic and learn of the consequences.

As a prelude to evangelism, poll your classmates and see how many of them believe in reincarnation.

Nail It Down: Compare the Hindu belief in reincarnation with Hebrews 9:27.

Pray About It:

∞ ∞ ∞ ∞ ∞ ∞   T W O

While waiting to get his hair cut, Tim is flipping through some magazines. One article that catches his eye is in a recent issue of People. It talks about singer Tina Turner, actor Richard Gere, and several other celebrities who have become Buddhists.

"Hmmm," he thinks. "Isn't Buddha the guy with the big, round belly?"

The guy with the big round belly

Look It Up: Buddhists believe that the goal of human existence is to escape from our world of suffering through *nirvana*—literally a "blowing out" of the flame of life along with its desires and passions.

Strict Buddhists often live moral, sacrificial lives. But their lifestyle calls to mind the people described in the Biblical phrase as "having a form of godliness but denying its power" (2 Timothy 3:5).

Furthermore, Buddhism rejects the need for God. It is based largely on human effort, which is an inadequate foundation. "For no one can lay any foundation other than the one already laid, which is Jesus Christ" (1 Corinthians 3:11).

Think It Through: The founder of Buddhism was Siddhartha Gautama who lived (scholars think) from 563 to 483 B.C. in what is now Nepal.

• The Buddhist scriptures are the *Tripitaka* and the *Dhammapada*.

• The word *Buddha* means "the enlightened one."

• Buddhism has two branches. *Theravada* is the oldest form. It declares enlightenment to be possible only for monks. *Mahayana* is more popular. It opens up the way of enlightenment to all.

• Like Hindus, Buddhists believe in reincarnation.

• Buddhism claims over 200 million followers.

Work It Out: Though their solutions are unsound, Buddhists rightly recognize the problems caused by human cravings and desires.

Are sinful urges running wild in your life? Are you doing things that may cause you great suffering (Galatians 6:7)? Turn away from those wrong thoughts and actions. Recommit yourself to the Lord.

Nail It Down: Read about the only true rescue from this evil age—Galatians 1:3-4.

∞ ∞ ∞ ∞ ∞ ∞ ∞ ∞ THREE **WORLD RELIGIONS**

On a downtown shopping trip, Esther, who is Jewish, and Candace happen upon a man who is standing on a busy sidewalk, playing the guitar, and singing at the top of his lungs. His shirt reads "Jews for Jesus." Next to him two people are handing out literature.

"Hey," Candace exclaims to Esther. "I didn't know you guys believed in Jesus."

"We don't," says Esther with a look of disapproval over her shoulder. "At least I don't."

What to think about the Jews

Look It Up: Devout Jews and Christians have much in common. Both believe in the holy, eternal, all-knowing, all-powerful God of the Bible. Both believe the Old Testament to be the Word of God.

The sharp difference between Christians and Jews is over the issue of Jesus of Nazareth. Judaism calls Him a great teacher, perhaps even a prophet. But Jesus claimed to be much more than that.

"The high priest said to [Jesus], 'I charge you under oath by the living God: Tell us if you are the Christ, the Son of God.'

" 'Yes, it is as you say,' Jesus replied" (Matthew 26:63-64).

Think It Through: The 12 million Jews in the world belong to three primary movements within Judaism: Orthodox, Reform, or Conservative.

Orthodox Jews strictly follow the Law. Reform Jews are more liberal, focusing less on particular rituals and more on broad ethics. Conservative Jews try to find a middle ground between the two.

A small percentage of Jews *do* recognize Jesus as the Messiah. These Jewish Christians are known as Messianic Jews.

Work It Out: Do you have Jewish friends or neighbors?

1. Pray for those individuals—that God would show them the truth about Jesus Christ.

2. Ask if you can attend synagogue with them. Then invite them to your church or youth group.

3. Don't condemn them. Instead, learn and show them the Old Testament prophecies Jesus fulfilled. Then tell them how Christ has changed your life.

Nail It Down: Would you say that Jesus fits the description of the Messiah prophesied in Isaiah 53?

Pray About It:

FOUR

∞ ∞ ∞ ∞ ∞ ∞ ∞

Look at all those "isms"!

Keith's head is spinning as he reads the unit on religion in his sociology book—Confucianism, Taoism, Shintoism, Jainism, Sikhism, Parsism, and a few pages on the various religious beliefs among tribal peoples.

"Whew!" he thinks, "Look at all these different religions. No matter where you go, someone else has a different 'ism'!"

Look It Up: What separates the various world religions from Biblical Christianity is the person of Jesus Christ.

• He is the only one who can make us right with God.

"Jesus answered, 'I am the way and the truth and the life. No one comes to the Father except through me'" (John 14:6).

"There is one God and one mediator between God and men, the man Christ Jesus" (1 Timothy 2:5).

• He alone died for the sins of mankind.

"At just the right time, when we were still powerless, Christ died for the ungodly" (Romans 5:6).

"What I received I passed on to you as of first importance: that Christ died for our sins according to the Scriptures" (1 Corinthians 15:3).

• Wise men and women listen to Him.

"Jesus answered, 'You are right in saying I am a king. In fact, for this reason I was born, and for this I came into the world, to testify to the truth. Everyone on the side of truth listens to me'" (John 18:37).

Think It Through: Read in the encyclopedia about one of the religions listed above. What, in your opinion, would attract people to it? How would you tell a person from that background about Christ?

Work It Out: Want to find out more about the various religions of the world? Check out *A Book of Beliefs* by John Allan, John Butterworth, and Myrtle Langley. Or consider *So What's the Difference* by Fritz Ridenour.

If you want to know how to respond to those with different beliefs, read *The Christian's Attitude Toward World Religions* by Ajith Fernando.

Nail It Down: Read 1 Peter 2:24. On Saturday, read Hebrews 9:11-28. For Sunday, read Matthew 7:15-23.

∘ ∞ ∞ ∞ ∞ ∞ ∞ ∞ FIVE **WORLD RELIGIONS** ∘

▲ ▲ ▲ ▲ SECRETS ▲ ▲ ▲ ▲ ▲
Do you want to know a secret?

Pssst! Can you keep a secret? Do you promise not to tell? I've never told anybody else this, but . . ."

Sometimes keeping secrets is good. Like when a friend shares something personal with you and you promise not to tell anyone else. But sometimes keeping secrets is *not* so good. Like when you've sinned—and you try to hide your sin from God. Or when you keep the Gospel secret from other people. Do you know when—and when not—to keep a secret?

"Your Father, who sees what is done in secret, will reward you" (Matthew 6:4).

Jeffrey steps out into the hallway, stops, and listens. The only noise in the whole house is coming from downstairs—the sound of his mom emptying the dishwasher. He tiptoes into his parents' bedroom. All clear.

Moving quickly over to his dad's dresser, Jeffrey quietly opens the bottom drawer. Sorting through the socks, he gingerly opens an old cigar box filled with silver dollars. Heart pounding, he removes four of the coins.

"Will he notice?" Jeffrey worries. "Nah, there's at least fifty left. But just to be safe, I'll put one back."

No secrets with God

Look It Up: We may be able to hide our evil thoughts and actions from people, but the Bible is clear that there are no secrets with God.

"If we had forgotten the name of our God or spread out our hands to a foreign god, would not God have discovered it, since he knows the secrets of the heart?" (Psalm 44:20-21).

"You have set our iniquities before you, our secret sins in the light of your presence" (Psalm 90:8).

Not only does God see our secret sins, He will also judge them one day. The apostle Paul, writing to the church at Rome, spoke of a coming day "when God will judge men's secrets through Jesus Christ, as my gospel declares" (Romans 2:16).

Think It Through: Are you involved in any "secret" activities such as

- cheating on tests at school;
- indulging in sexual activities;
- shoplifting or stealing;
- sneaking around behind your parents' backs;
- looking at pornographic magazines or videos?

Does it make you feel guilty to know that God clearly sees your secret thoughts and actions?

Work It Out: If you answered yes to any of those questions (especially the last one) the solution is clear. You need to take these three steps:

1. Admit to God that your actions are wrong (1 John 1:9).

2. Tell God that you want to change and that you need His strength to do so (Philippians 4:13).

3. Find a Christian friend in whom you can confide and who will agree to help you to overcome your "not-so-secret" sins (James 5:16-20).

Nail It Down: Read Jeremiah 23:23-24.

▲▲▲▲▲▲ ᴼᴺᴱ **SECRETS** ▲▲▲▲▲▲

"Brittany, are you coming to K. D.'s party Saturday night?"

Brittany rolls her eyes. "I've got more important things to do."

"Huh? What could be more important than a party?"

Brittany gets a proud look on her face. "Well for starters there's the youth group food drive. But of course you wouldn't dare give up one night of your precious time to do something nice for somebody else!"

It's time to join the secret service!

Look It Up: The Bible tells us not to make a big show of our good works.

"Be careful not to do your 'acts of righteousness' before men, to be seen by them. If you do, you will have no reward from your Father in heaven.

"So when you give to the needy, do not announce it with trumpets, as the hypocrites do in the synagogues and on the streets, to be honored by men. I tell you the truth, they have received their reward in full. But when you give to the needy, do not let your left hand know what your right hand is doing, so that your giving may be in secret. Then your Father, who sees what is done in secret, will reward you.

"And when you pray, do not be like the hypocrites, for they love to pray standing in the synagogues and on the street corners to be seen by men. I tell you the truth, they have received their reward in full. But when you pray, go into your room, close the door and pray to your Father, who is unseen. Then your Father, who sees what is done in secret, will reward you" (Matthew 6:1-6).

Think It Through: Why is it so hard to do something nice for someone and keep your mouth shut about it?

Work It Out: Join God's "secret service" today.
• When no one is looking, quietly do a job around the house that needs to be done.
• Write your favorite teacher an anonymous encouraging note.
• Give to a worthy cause (a missionary, a food drive, a family in trouble) without telling anyone.

Nail It Down: Read about the bad motives behind the Pharisees' good deeds—Matthew 23:5-7.

Pray About It:

▲▲▲▲▲ TWO

157

Meredith is in the thick of a messy, mixed-up situation. She feels like her parents wouldn't understand, and she doesn't dare discuss such an important matter with Melinda. (If she did, her problem would be all over the school by lunch time!)

Meredith finally decides to talk with Amy after school. She reasons, "The secrets I've shared with Amy in the past have never gotten back to me. I think I can trust her to keep her mouth shut."

Can you keep a secret?

Look It Up: Wise King Solomon repeatedly warned against breaking a confidence—against being a blabbermouth like Melinda.

• "A gossip betrays a confidence, but a trustworthy man keeps a secret" (Proverbs 11:13).

• "A perverse man stirs up dissension, and a gossip separates close friends" (Proverbs 16:28).

• "He who covers over an offense promotes love, but whoever repeats the matter separates close friends" (Proverbs 17:9).

Think It Through: Have you ever shared a deep, dark secret with someone only to find out later that your confidant told about 500 folks? It's a rotten feeling, isn't it?

What about you? Are you more like Amy or Melinda? That is, can people trust you with their secrets? Or, is confiding in you like broadcasting over the school P.A. system? Put it this way: How would you feel if others kept your secrets to the same extent that you keep theirs?

Work It Out: If you have a reputation as a motormouth, make it a point today to apologize to anyone whose confidence you have violated. Simply say, "Hey, you told me _____ , and I said I wouldn't tell, but I did. I was wrong. I'm sorry. It will never happen again. Will you please forgive me?"

Then work hard to become known as a person who keeps his or her word. If you tell someone your lips are sealed, don't break your promise!

And if you know you'll be tempted to blab a certain secret, don't even let yourself hear the information that is confidential.

Nail It Down: Be careful not to share your secrets with a gossip— see Proverbs 20:19.

▲▲▲▲▲▲ THREE SECRETS ▲▲▲▲▲▲

Russ is eating pizza with a few of the guys from the football team. Suddenly one of them remarks, "Watch out! Holy Joe just arrived."

Russ looks up and notices Joe Rogers, his youth leader, talking to some students. Immediately Russ's buddies start with the wise-cracks and put-downs.

Russ knows he should stick up for Joe and even let his teammates know where he stands, but he can't seem to get up the nerve. In fact, when Joe looks over toward the players, Russ looks away to avoid making eye contact!

▲▲▲▲▲ **FOUR**

No more secret disciples!

Look It Up: Following Jesus secretly is not a new trend.
• "Yet at the same time many even among the leaders believed in him [Jesus]. But because of the Pharisees they would not confess their faith for fear they would be put out of the synagogue; for they loved praise from men more than praise from God" (John 12:42-43).
• "Later, Joseph of Arimathea asked Pilate for the body of Jesus. Now Joseph was a disciple of Jesus, but secretly because he feared the Jews. With Pilate's permission, he came and took the body away. He was accompanied by Nicodemus, the man who earlier had visited Jesus at night" (John 19:38-39).

Think It Through: Can you relate to Russ's situation? How might you react in a similar setting? Why is it so hard sometimes to stand up for Jesus Christ?

Work It Out: Take a step today to let others know about your faith in Jesus Christ. First, pray for boldness. Second, try one or more of the following:
1. Invite a friend to church.
2. Take a Bible or a Christian magazine to school.
3. Encourage a non-Christian friend to listen to your favorite Christian tape.
4. Look for natural opportunities to talk about what you believe. Then —without being preachy— simply share what Christ means to you.
5. Talk openly about the things your youth group is doing.
6. Join a Christian club at your school. (If there isn't one, start one!)

Nail It Down: Read about the danger of being a secret disciple—Matthew 10:32-33.

Pray About It:

Last summer Joy went on a mission trip and led four people to Christ. This fall she has played a big part in seeing two of her best friends put their faith in Jesus.

How can she be so bold?

"I don't think of myself as bold. Just blessed. I mean, if I found the cure for cancer, you can bet I'd tell everyone I met. Well, I have found the cure for cancer—for spiritual cancer. How could I keep that to myself?"

Get excited and tell everybody!

Look It Up: During one especially bleak period of her history, Israel was in the midst of a war and a horrible famine.

"Now there were four men with leprosy at the entrance of the city gate. They said to each other, 'Why stay here until we die? If we say, "We'll go into the city"—the famine is there, and we will die. And if we stay here, we will die. So let's go over to the camp of the Arameans and surrender. If they spare us, we live; if they kill us, then we die'" (2 Kings 7:3-4).

Imagine their surprise when the men discovered the enemy camp deserted! God had caused the Arameans to flee in the night—leaving behind all their food and supplies! The lepers celebrated their good fortune until this thought hit them: "We're not doing right. This is a day of good news and we are keeping it to ourselves. . . . Let's go at once and report this to the royal palace" (2 Kings 7:9).

Think It Through: Some things need to be kept confidential, but not good news. Good news is for sharing!

Are you keeping the good news of God's love to yourself?

Work It Out: Start telling others the story about Christ's love for the world and His death on the cross.

Buy a variety of gospel tracts at your local Christian bookstore. Give them to friends and say something like, "Hey, this booklet summarizes what I believe about God. Tell me what you think about it. Look it over and let's discuss it tomorrow, okay?"

Then pray like crazy and watch God work!

Nail It Down: Read Acts 1:8. On Saturday, read Romans 1:14-17. On Sunday, read through and think about Romans 10:13-15.

▲▲▲▲▲▲ FIVE SECRETS ▲▲▲▲▲▲

DEATH
God in the graveyard

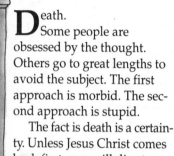

Death.
Some people are obsessed by the thought. Others go to great lengths to avoid the subject. The first approach is morbid. The second approach is stupid.

The fact is death is a certainty. Unless Jesus Christ comes back first, you will die at a precise moment in the future. Maybe not for a long time . . . or maybe sooner than you think. But you will die.

So get ready now. Because you can't really live until you're ready to die.

"Like water spilled on the ground, which cannot be recovered, so we must die" (2 Samuel 14:14).

Pat and his friends like to live on the edge—to see how much speed and danger they can pack into each weekend.

That's why they waterski at night and rev the boat up to full throttle and take turns jumping out! That's the same reason they go cave exploring after dark.

Try talking to Pat seriously about calming down his daredevil lifestyle or about the possibility of serious injury or death, and he just laughs.

"Die? Man, I'm gonna live to be 120!"

The myth of immortality

Look It Up: There are many subjects about which Scripture is unclear; however, death is not one of them. When it comes to the topic of mortality, the Bible plainly says that all people will die.

• "What man can live and not see death, or save himself from the power of the grave?" (Psalm 89:48).

• "All go to the same place; all come from dust, and to dust all return" (Ecclesiastes 3:20).

• "No man has power over the wind to contain it; so no one has power over the day of his death" (Ecclesiastes 8:8).

Think It Through: A few questions for you—

1. Do you think most of your friends really believe they are going to die?

2. Why are people so sad at funerals?

3. Have you ever had to endure the loss of a family member or close friend? (If so, how did you react?)

4. Why are most people afraid of death?

Work It Out: Try one of these experiments:

Get a copy of your local newspaper and locate the obituary page. Note the ages of the deceased. Most were probably elderly, but if you live in a larger city, you may find a notice describing the death of someone younger—perhaps even a teenager. How does that make you feel?

With a friend or two, walk through a local cemetery. Read some of the grave stones. Look for people who lived long lives. Look for others who died at young ages. Imagine what their lives were like, and what they were doing when they drew their last breath. Think about your own life and how much time you may (or may not) have left.

Nail It Down: Read Job 30:23 and Psalm 49:10.

▶▶▶▶▶▶▶ ONE **DEATH** ▶▶▶▶▶▶▶▶▶

On a recent visit to see her sister in medical school, 16-year-old Jenny sneaked into the "cadaver room" where all the first-year medical students learn human anatomy by working on real-life (or is it real-death?) corpses.

The room reeked of formaldehyde, and the cut-up cadavers looked less like human remains and more like picked-over turkey carcasses.

"I just saw that one's arm move!" Jenny screamed.

"Jenny!" Patricia chided. "Don't be ridiculous! They're dead, silly!"

A deeper, darker kind of death

Look It Up: According to the Bible, humans don't just face physical death; we also, until we trust in Jesus, experience a deeper, darker type of spiritual death.

• "'But we had to celebrate and be glad, because this brother of yours was dead and is alive again; he was lost and is found'" (Luke 15:32).

• "'If you do not believe that I [Jesus] am the one I claim to be, you will indeed die in your sins'" (John 8:24).

• "As for you, you were dead in your transgressions and sins" (Ephesians 2:1).

• "When you were dead in your sins and in the uncircumcision of your sinful nature, God made you alive with Christ" (Colossians 2:13).

Think It Through: The verses you just read mean that many of the people you sit with in class, pass in traffic, watch football games with, and live near in the neighborhood are dead. Cut off from the spiritual life that only Christ can bring, these individuals are walking, talking, corpses! They're like zombies, and once their bodies quit working, they'll face eternity—separated from God!

Work It Out: Do something today to help a spiritually dead person find new life in Christ.

1. Loan out your favorite Christian tape.
2. Invite someone to youth group.
3. Share your testimony with a classmate.
4. Introduce your non-Christian friends to your youth leader.
5. Do some serious praying for an unbelieving parent or teacher.

Nail It Down: Read Ephesians 5:8-14.

Pray About It:

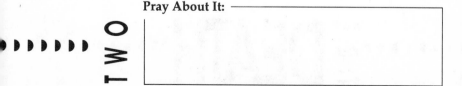

TWO

163

Woody's family is just amazed by a news story about a man who was shocked by more than 7,000 volts of electricity, pronounced dead, covered with a sheet, and was then discovered breathing some forty minutes later by an orderly in the hospital morgue.

"What a miracle!" blurts Woody.

"I wonder where he spent those forty minutes," jokes Woody's mom. "Either he is very relieved or very sad to be back from the dead!"

Life beyond the grave

Look It Up: It's hard to explain modern-day stories of people who have reportedly "died" and come back to life. Are they miracles? Mysteries? Medical mistakes? No one can say for sure. But the fact of an afterlife is crystal clear:

• "'I tell you the truth, if anyone keeps my word, he will never see death'" (John 8:51).

• "Jesus said to her, 'I am the resurrection and the life. He who believes in me will live, even though he dies; and whoever lives and believes in me will never die. Do you believe this?' " (John 11:25-26).

• "Our Savior, Christ Jesus . . . has destroyed death and has brought life and immortality to light through the gospel" (2 Timothy 1:10).

Think It Through: Yesterday we looked at two kinds of death. Today we're seeing that there are two kinds of life.

Physical existence is in the here and now. But for believers in Christ, a life beyond this world awaits them —a life that is far too awesome for words.

What do you think life will be like after our bodies die? Why? Are your ideas about heaven based on the Bible or something else?

Work It Out: Write a short note to someone in your school or church who is grieving over the loss of a loved one. Don't offer canned advice, spout simplistic clichés, or quote reams of Scripture. (Grieving people need helping hands and listening ears—not lecturing tongues!) Simply assure the individual that you are thinking of and praying for him or her.

(If you are grieving right now, seek out a mature Christian for emotional and spiritual support.)

Nail It Down: Read 1 Corinthians 15:35-57.

▶▶▶▶▶▶ **THREE DEATH** ▶▶▶▶▶▶▶▶▶

Yesterday afternoon Chip attended the funeral of his grandmother. It was like a huge, depressing family reunion—dozens of aunts, uncles, and cousins filling the church, many of them sobbing out of control.

"I don't get it," Chip sighs. "Grandma was a Christian, so now she's in heaven. She's no longer in pain, right? Yet all those people were crying their eyes out, like her death is the worst thing in the world!

"Don't get me wrong—I'm gonna miss her too. But if what we believe is true, then she's a lot happier now."

The death of a saint ain't awful!

Look It Up: Chip's on the right track. Death may be sad for those who get left behind. But it's like graduation to the Christian who is going on to be with the Lord! Even in death

• God sees—"Precious in the sight of the LORD is the death of his saints" (Psalm 116:15);

• God protects—"When calamity comes, the wicked are brought down, but even in death the righteous have a refuge" (Proverbs 14:32);

• God promises security—"If we live, we live to the Lord; and if we die, we die to the Lord. So, whether we live or die, we belong to the Lord" (Romans 14:8).

Think It Through: Which is more difficult? To face the sudden, unexpected death of a loved one? Or to watch a friend or family member experience a long and painful terminal illness?

If you could plan your own funeral, would you want it to be a somber, depressing occasion or more of a celebration? Why?

Work It Out: Find out more about the afterlife by doing a quick study in the book of Revelation. List what each of these passages tells us about heaven:

1. Revelation 14:13 _____

_____

2. Revelation 21:1-4 _____

_____

3. Revelation 22:1-5 _____

_____

_____

Nail It Down: Read Philippians 1:21.

Pray About It:

FOUR

Walter is sharing his faith in Christ with a young man at a downtown bus stop. Let's listen in on their conversation.

"So you don't know what's going to happen to you when you die?"

"Well, I hope I'll go to heaven, but I don't know."

"Would you like to see what the Bible says, how you can know for sure?"

" 'For sure?' I don't believe anyone can know 'for sure.' I think we all just have to wait till we die and then see."

Are you prepared?

Look It Up: Hey, there's no need to wonder about eternal life. If you believe the Word of God, you can know right now what is waiting for you after death. See?

• "'I tell you the truth, whoever hears my word and believes him who sent me has eternal life and will not be condemned; he has crossed over from death to life'" (John 5:24).

• "For the wages of sin is death, but the gift of God is eternal life in Christ Jesus our Lord" (Romans 6:23).

• "He who has the Son has life; he who does not have the Son of God does not have life. I write these things to you who believe in the name of the Son of God so that you may know that you have eternal life" (1 John 5:12-13).

Think It Through: There's a saying that goes like this:

"Born once and you die twice; born twice and you die once."

Do you understand what that means?

Have you been born twice?

Work It Out: If you have any doubts at all about your destination after death, now is the time to resolve them.

The verses in the "Look It Up" section on this page explain that eternal life is a gift to everyone who trusts in Christ. They aren't just empty words, they are promises from the very mouth of God.

The moment we believe in Christ, the moment we receive His gift of eternal life, God says we can know (1 John 5:13) for sure that we are headed for heaven. No guesswork. No hoping or wondering. We can be sure because the promises of God can be trusted.

If you've never trusted in Christ alone to forgive your sins, do so right now.

Nail It Down: Read 1 John 5:1. On Saturday, read John 3:1-16. On Sunday, read 1 Peter 1:23-25.

▷▷▷▷▷▷▷ FIVE **DEATH** ▷▷▷▷▷▷▷▷▷

HELL

You have probably heard people mention hell in expressions like: *life is hell; it's hotter than hell;* or *go to hell*. Possibly you've heard someone say that heaven sounds boring, so hell must be the opposite—an outrageous celebration where you party with your friends for eternity. Maybe you've heard someone say that hell doesn't exist.

Despite such wishful thinking, there's no getting around this truth: *Jesus clearly taught about a real place called hell* (Matthew 5:22-30; Luke 16:19-31).

What is Hell like? Most of us, when we really think about hell, conjure up a grim picture of little red devils running around, poking and jabbing their screaming victims with pitchforks. But what are the facts?

The Bible tells us three main things about the future state of the unbeliever. First, hell will be *eternal*. It will last forever (Matthew 25:46). Second, hell will be *punishment for sin and unbelief* (2 Thessalonians 1:8). Third, hell will be *separation from God* (2 Thessalonians 1:9).

Death is not nothingness. Revelation 21:8 describes hell as "the second death." In the Bible death always refers to physical or spiritual *separation* (not nothingness). So, while the first death will be the physical separation from life, the second death will be the eternal and spiritual separation from the source of life—God. In short, heaven will be eternal life for the believer. Hell will be eternal death for the unbeliever.

The British writer C. S. Lewis summed it up when he said that sin is man saying to God throughout life, "Go away and leave me alone," and hell is God finally saying to man, "You may have your wish," and leaving him to himself for eternity.

What should believers do? First, we must realize that life is a serious matter and the stakes are high, because human lives are involved. Second, we need to share our faith with unbelievers. People around us are sick with sin and we have the cure to their spiritual disease. Third, when we realize how horrible hell really is—*an eternal separation from God*—it should compel us to thank God for saving us. We would all be doomed to a terrible destiny if not for His loving grace.

THE CASE OF A MISTAKEN IDENTITY

If people believed things about you that were totally untrue, you'd want to set the record straight, wouldn't you?

That's the purpose of this page—to tell the truth about who God really is. Understand that He doesn't need us to defend Him. But at the same time, He is glorified when we try to clear up the wrong ideas others may have.

The Popular Misconception

1. *The Indifferent Landlord*—God is too busy to care about our little problems. We never hear from Him —unless we fail to pay the rent!

2. *The Impatient Teacher*—God shakes His head and rolls His eyes every time we do the least little thing wrong. He's always telling His angels what dunces we are.

3. *The Cosmic Policeman*—God is on His beat . . . hoping for the chance to beat up anyone having any fun in life.

4. *The Absent-minded Professor*—God is the well-meaning, but "in over His head" deity who can't control things.

5. *The Chameleon*—God is whatever you want Him to be.

6. *The Sentimental Grandpa*—God is the mischievous old man with a twinkle in His eye, who looks the other way when we get rambunctious and wild.

What the Bible Really Says

1. God is actively involved in the world and in our lives (Romans 8:28). He cares deeply for us (1 Peter 5:7).

2. God is perfectly patient (2 Peter 3:9) and gentle. Whenever we fall, He is right there to pick us up (Psalm 37:24).

3. God longs for us to find a life in Him that is rich and satisfying (John 10:10).

4. God is in complete control because He has all power (Psalm 115:3).

5. God is who He is—not a deity we can design (Exodus 3:14).

6. God is holy and cannot overlook sin (Psalm 99:9).

POPULARITY
How favor affects your faith

Popularity seems like such a good thing. You walk down the hall and people smile and greet you by name. Behind your back, they say nice things about you. Popularity means lots of invitations and phone calls; it means being selected by your peers for honors, awards, and applause.

But is popularity all it's cracked up to be? Before you answer too quickly, perhaps you need to read the following five pages.

"Woe to you when all men speak well of you, for that is how their fathers treated the false prophets" (Luke 6:26).

Melissa can't stand Kaycee, a classmate who lives up the street. Kaycee is very popular. Not only is she a senior class officer, but she also was recently elected Homecoming Queen.

"What has she got that I haven't got? I'm a nice person too. I'm not bad looking. Why don't I ever get any honors like that?"

Meanwhile Kaycee is beginning her campaign to try to get a date with Kurt (the school heart throb).

The power and pull of popularity

Look It Up: Popularity is dangerous for at least two reasons.

1. It can become a major source of jealousy.

"When Saul saw how successful he [David] was, he was afraid of him. But all Israel and Judah loved David, because he led them in their campaigns" (1 Samuel 18:15-16).

2. It can become an obsession.

"So he [Haman] answered the king, 'For the man the king delights to honor, have them bring a royal robe the king has worn and a horse the king has ridden, one with a royal crest placed on its head. Then let the robe and horse be entrusted to one of the king's most noble princes. Let them robe the man the king delights to honor, and lead him on the horse through the city streets, proclaiming before him, "This is what is done for the man the king delights to honor!" ' " (Esther 6:7-9).

Think It Through: Like Melissa, are you jealous of someone at school who is popular? Do you ever catch yourself doing certain things just to make others think more highly of you? After such feelings and/or actions, do you feel better or worse about yourself?

Work It Out: Ask God to give you a handle on this week's topic. If you aren't especially popular among your peers, ask Him to give you needed insights and proper attitudes.

If you are part of the popular crowd, ask the Lord to keep you from getting a big head. Then, with the help of a Christian friend, analyze your behavior for any actions that might not be pleasing to God.

Nail It Down: Observe in John 3:25-30 how John the Baptist dealt with his lessening popularity—and the increasing popularity of Christ.

★ ★ ★ ★ ★ ★ ONE **POPULARITY** ★ ★

W ell, are you coming or not?"

Rod wavers, staring at the ground, as five pairs of demanding eyes focus impatiently on him.

(The six guys just got invited to watch some hardcore porno videos at a college frat house.)

"No," Rod finally mumbles. As the guys turn to go, he hears them saying, "The guy must be gay or something!" and, "I thought Rod was cool!"

"Right" is never easy

Look It Up: Rod's story echoes what happened in Numbers 13 when the Israeli spies returned from Canaan. The majority of the men swayed the people with their negative report, "We can't attack those people; they are stronger than we are" (v. 31).

After a night of national complaining and weeping, "Joshua son of Nun and Caleb son of Jephunneh, who were among those who had explored the land, tore their clothes and said to the entire Israelite assembly, 'The land we passed through and explored is exceedingly good. If the LORD is pleased with us, he will lead us into that land . . . and will give it to us. Only do not rebel against the LORD. And do not be afraid of the people of the land, because we will swallow them up. Their protection is gone, but the LORD is with us. Do not be afraid of them.'

"But the whole assembly talked about stoning them" (Numbers 14:6-10).

Think It Through: God expects His people to stand up for the truth. Could you have done what Rod did? What Joshua and Caleb did? Why or why not?

Work It Out: Choose to do the right thing today. For example,
• when others are dogging someone, stand up for him/her;
• when classmates encourage you to cheat, say no;
• when it seems like "everyone is doing it"— whether "it" is cursing, doing drugs, drinking, having sex, shoplifting, or whatever—pray for the courage to stand alone!

Nail It Down: Read about the apostles who chose obedience over the approval of others—Acts 4:18-20 and Acts 5:25-29.

Pray About It:

T W O

Nora wanted so badly to be part of the "in" group. And she thought she had the perfect plan to get in—a party for all the popular crowd while her parents were away for the weekend.

Here's the result of Nora's "perfect plan": On Saturday morning, the house is trashed, the VCR is broken, some jewelry is missing. Worst of all, Nora's virginity is long gone.

Panting for popularity

Look It Up: During the time of King David, two guys named Recab and Baanah murdered a guy named Ish-Bosheth. They cut off his head and took it to David thinking they would win favor with him:

"David answered Recab and his brother Baanah . . . , 'As surely as the LORD lives, who has delivered me out of all trouble, when a man told me, "Saul is dead," and thought he was bringing good news, I seized him and put him to death in Ziklag. That was the reward I gave him for his news! How much more—when wicked men have killed an innocent man in his own house and on his own bed—should I not now demand his blood from your hand . . . !'

"So David gave an order to his men, and they killed them. They cut off their hands and feet and hung the bodies by the pool in Hebron. But they took the head of Ish-Bosheth and buried it in Abner's tomb at Hebron" (2 Samuel 4:9-12).

Think It Through: Do you agree or disagree with the following statement? "People who make you work for their friendship are not worth having as friends."

Have you ever tried to get on someone's good side only to have things blow up in your face?

Work It Out: Make the following personal commitments today:

1. I will not try to be someone or something I'm not.
2. I will not try to earn the acceptance of others. If certain "friends" won't accept me for who and what I am, then I'll find new friends.
3. I will not pressure others into feeling like they have to perform in order to be on my good side.

Nail It Down: Read 2 Samuel 1:1-16 for another popularity plan that went poof!

★ ★ ★ ★ ★ ★ THREE **POPULARITY** ★ ★

Rod (see story on Day 2) is shocked. In only two days' time, his reputation has done a 180 degree turn. On Tuesday he was a fairly popular guy. Today, he can hardly get anyone to speak to him.

Oh, a few friends from church have whispered that they are proud of the stand he took, but everyone else has totally deserted him.

When the cheers turn to jeers

Look It Up: Jesus knew the highs and lows of popularity. Early in His ministry, He was the toast of the town.

"Jesus withdrew with his disciples to the lake, and a large crowd from Galilee followed. When they heard all he was doing, many people came to him from Judea, Jerusalem, Idumea, and the regions across the Jordan" (Mark 3:7-8).

Even when he entered Jerusalem for the final time, he had a high approval rating.

"Those who went ahead and those who followed shouted, 'Hosanna! Blessed is he who comes in the name of the Lord! Blessed is the coming kingdom of our father David! Hosanna in the highest!' " (Mark 11:9-10).

But consider the public's opinion of Christ only a few days later.

" 'What shall I do, then, with the one you call the king of the Jews?' Pilate asked them.

" 'Crucify him!' they shouted" (Mark 15:12-13).

Think It Through: Popularity is a fickle thing. One day everyone loves you. The next day your world crashes in.

If you base your self-worth solely on the opinion of others, will you experience stability or anxiety?

Work It Out: Have the cheers turned to jeers in your life? Take comfort in these facts:

• The world only mocks when you're doing what is right.

• Jesus knows exactly how you feel.

• No one is popular with everyone all the time.

• God promises strength to face your situation (Philippians 4:13).

Nail It Down: Read more about the shaky popularity of Jesus—John 12:9-10.

Pray About It:

★ ★ ★ ★ ★ FOUR

The big fall outreach that Marci and her youth group have been planning for two months turned out to be, so it seems, a huge bust.

Twenty-seven kids showed up, and all of them were already believers in Jesus.

"I don't get it," Marci moans. "We prayed, we advertised, we worked so hard. Why can't we get non-Christians interested in the gospel?"

Why the gospel isn't more popular

Look It Up: You'd think that people would be lining up to trust Christ . . . scrambling like mad to know that their sins were forgiven and that their eternal destiny was secure, but it doesn't work that way.

The gospel message isn't very popular because
• it demands that we acknowledge our need for the spiritual healing that only Christ can bring (Matthew 9:11-13);
• until God opens a person's heart, it is impossible to fully comprehend (1 Corinthians 2:14);
• embracing it completely will lead to hardship and persecution: "This is my gospel, for which I am suffering even to the point of being chained like a criminal. . . . You, however, know all about my . . . persecutions, sufferings—what kinds of things happened to me in Antioch, Iconium and Lystra, the persecutions I endured. Yet the Lord rescued me from all of them. In fact, everyone who wants to live a godly life in Christ Jesus will be persecuted (2 Timothy 2:8-9, 3:10-12).

Think It Through: In what specific ways is the message of Christ's death on the cross "foolish?" (See 1 Corinthians 1:18-29.)

Work It Out: God has called us to share the story of Christ's love regardless of how people respond. Ask Him for an opportunity to do that today. Then be sensitive to the Spirit's leading. Who knows? You may see a miracle!

Nail It Down: Read about the religious leaders who were jealous of Jesus' popularity—John 9:13-17. On Saturday, reflect on the manner with which Jesus regarded His popularity—John 2:23-25. On Sunday, contemplate the fleeting popularity enjoyed by Jesus' followers in Matthew 5:1-2.

★ ★ ★ ★ ★ ★ FIVE **POPULARITY** ★ ★

MARRIAGE
Matrimony without the alimony

It's been said that marriage is the only institution on earth in which everyone on the outside wants in, and everyone on the inside wants out!

That crack is an obvious exaggeration, but since most people do eventually get married (some people more than once), and since marriage has the potential to be either a wonderful experience or a horrible nightmare, we thought it might be wise to hear from the One who thought the whole thing up.

"Marriage should be honored by all" (Hebrews 13:4).

Angie is adamant. "No way! I'm never getting married. Not after watching how my parents treat each other."

"But, Angie, just because your parents had a bad experience and divorced doesn't mean that you have to follow in their footsteps. You can still have a really good marriage one day."

"Nope. It isn't worth the risk. Too many of my friends tell the same horror stories. I'm not going to put myself through all that mess."

Marriage: Why the bad rap?

Look It Up: The way people talk and act, you'd think that marriage is the worst idea anyone ever came up with. But listen to King Solomon—a man who had more than 700 wives:

"He who finds a wife finds what is good and receives favor from the LORD" (Proverbs 18:22).

And listen to this encouragement from the apostle Paul, a bachelor who helped lead the early church:

"A deacon must be the husband of but one wife and must manage his children and his household well" (1 Timothy 3:12).

"So I counsel younger widows to marry, to have children, to manage their homes and to give the enemy no opportunity for slander" (1 Timothy 5:14).

Think It Through: When we hear about a quack doctor, we don't decide that medical principles are suddenly invalid. And when an airplane crashes, we don't conclude that the laws of aeronautics no longer work.

So how come when a lot of people bail out of their marriages, we write marriage off as a bad deal?

Is the institution of marriage defective, or are the people involved defective?

Work It Out: Don't let our warped and twisted culture brainwash you into believing that marriage doesn't work. Marriage does work—amazingly well—when we follow the principles God has given us in His Word.

Ask God to open your spiritual eyes and spiritual ears to the truth about Christian marriage. (And begin now praying that, if it is His will for you to marry, God will prepare you and your potential mate for each other and His service.)

Nail It Down: Read God's command to the Hebrews who were in exile—Jeremiah 29:6. Then read verse 11. Does God picture marriage as a horrible deal?

ONE **MARRIAGE** ❤ ❤

When the phone rang just after dinner last night, Blair knew it was her friend Jenny. (So did everyone, since Jenny has called Blair just after dinner every night for two months!)

Blair did not expect what Jenny had to say:

"No!" she screamed in utter shock. "Mr. and Mrs. Brooks are getting a divorce? They've been married for almost 20 years!"

The next day, as Blair was driving to the mall, she thought about the phone call. "Well, I guess 20 years is a long time. Who knows? Maybe it's the best thing for the kids."

Marriage is for life!

Look It Up: From the very beginning, God meant for marriage to last.

"For this reason a man will leave his father and mother and be united to his wife, and they will become one flesh" (Genesis 2:24).

Jesus Christ, commenting on this verse, added, "So they are no longer two, but one. Therefore what God has joined together, let man not separate" (Mark 10:8-9).

And the Apostle Paul charged,

A wife must not separate from her husband. But if she does, she must remain unmarried or else be reconciled to her husband. And a husband must not divorce his wife" (1 Corinthians 7:10-11).

Think It Through: Some Christians interpret the Bible as teaching, "No divorce for any reason." Others insist that God permits divorce in cases of marital unfaithfulness. Still others allow divorce for other reasons such as abandonment or abuse.

Views on remarriage are just as diverse.

Use a concordance to look up the words *marry*, *marriage*, and *divorce*. What Scripture verses support (as well as undermine) your position?

Work It Out: If your parents are separated, pray fervently that their problems might be resolved and that your family might be restored.

If your parents are divorced, determine that by God's grace, you won't make the same mistakes.

If you have a friend whose family is in a divorce battle right now, take him or her out for pizza. Be a listening ear and a shoulder to cry on.

Nail It Down: Read the strong statement about divorce found in Malachi 2:13-16.

Pray About It:

TWO

People accuse Mark of being too picky about girls.

"Why so particular, Mark?"

"I don't want to get involved with the wrong person. I know that if I'm not careful, I could very well fall in love with someone who's not even a Christian. Then where would I be?"

"Mark, chill out! We're not talking about marriage here—just a simple date for the weekend!"

"Hey, I want to develop good habits now. I'm only 17, but one of these days, I hope to marry one of the girls I'm dating."

Picky, picky, picky!

Look It Up: Mark's a perceptive guy! It pays to be picky when it comes to the opposite sex, because marriage is a serious proposition. And being married to the wrong person can be a nightmare.

• "A quarrelsome wife is like a constant dripping" (Proverbs 19:13).

• "Better to live on a corner of the roof than share a house with a quarrelsome wife" (Proverbs 21:9).

• "Better to live in a desert than with a quarrelsome and ill-tempered wife" (Proverbs 21:19).

And don't forget—it isn't just women who cause problems in marriage. Guys can be real jerks too. So don't be in a rush to get hitched, girls.

Think It Through: Many Christians believe that God has one perfect person for you to marry, and that everyone else is less than the best. Others feel strongly that there are a wide variety of possible mates for each believer.

Which view do you hold? Why?

Work It Out: If you have never done so, sit down and write out some dating standards for yourself. Think about these questions, do some serious Bible study, then talk them over with your parents and/or youth leader.

1. Should I go out with non-Christians?
2. How far should I go physically on a date?
3. Is it right to date just one person?
4. What is the best age for marriage?
5. What is my purpose for dating?
6. What dangers should I avoid in dating?

Nail It Down: Read about the exiles with messed-up marriages and what they did to solve the problem—Ezra 9-10.

THREE **MARRIAGE**

Terry has been to some wild weddings in her 15 years, but none as amazing as the one she attended last weekend.

The father of the bride spent $10,000 just on flowers! He also had an entire orchestra flown in from a city 250 miles away to provide music for the occasion.

After the wedding there was an elegant sit-down dinner with prime rib and lobster for everyone! Then the newlyweds left in a helicopter for a three-week honeymoon at a secluded tropical paradise.

"It doesn't get any better than that," Terry sighed.

The wildest wedding of all!

Look It Up: Oh yes it does! According to the Bible, there will one day be a cosmic wedding ceremony even more amazing than the extravaganza Terry attended.

It is hinted at in the Old Testament:

"For your Maker is your husband—the LORD Almighty is his name—the Holy One of Israel is your Redeemer; he is called the God of all the earth" (Isaiah 54:5).

It is mentioned in the gospels:

"The kingdom of heaven is like a king who prepared a wedding banquet for his son" (Matthew 22:2).

It is described in the last book of the Bible:

"Let us rejoice and be glad and give him glory! For the wedding of the Lamb has come, and his bride has made herself ready" (Revelation 19:7).

Think It Through: What is the meaning of this "wedding of the Lamb?" No one knows all the details (the Bible doesn't tell us). All we know is that in some mysterious way, the Lamb of God, Jesus Christ, will "marry" His bride (that is, the people who belong to Him).

Are you part of the bride of Christ?

If so, are you being a faithful fiancée?

Work It Out: Invite at least one person to the ultimate wedding today. Confused?

Here's what we mean. Share the good news of Jesus Christ with a friend.

1. Pray for an opportunity and for the words to say.

2. Talk about Jesus (what He has done and is doing in your life).

3. Encourage a response. ("Would you like to trust Him to forgive your sins too?")

Nail It Down: Will individuals be married in heaven? See Matthew 22:30.

Pray About It:

♥ ♥ ♥ ♥ FOUR

During a psychology lecture, Dr. Carnell asked, "How many of you feel that premarital sex is wrong?"

Of 30 students, only Wendy raised her hand. Later, Shannon approached Wendy. "I can't believe you were so bold. I mean, I feel the same way you do about sex, but I guess I wimped out during class."

Save yourself for the big day!

Look It Up: We don't have to feel embarrassed about the decision to save sex for marriage—that's God's plan.

• "It is God's will that you should . . . avoid sexual immorality; that each of you should learn to control his own body in a way that is holy and honorable, not in passionate lust like the heathen, who do not know God; and that in this matter no one should wrong his brother or take advantage of him.

. . . For God did not call us to be impure, but to live a holy life" (1 Thessalonians 4:3-7).

• "Marriage should be honored by all, and the marriage bed kept pure, for God will judge the adulterer and all the sexually immoral" (Hebrews 13:4).

Think It Through: People who are sexually involved before marriage are stealing from their own futures.

Experiences that can have only one "first-time" are thoughtlessly given up in a moment of passion. And rather than being beautiful, tender, and special, those acts become bitter memories that we'd rather forget.

Premarital sex may feel good at the moment, but saving sex for marriage brings long-term pleasure.

Work It Out: For a more thorough look at all aspects of marriage (including discussions of "When is the right time?" and "Why not just live together?") read John Souter's *Marry*. *Marry* is a book that looks like a magazine. A product of Tyndale House Publishers, this creative (and a little bit crazy) publication will make you laugh and think at the same time.

Nail It Down: Read about the different responsibilities for husbands and wives in Ephesians 5:22-33. On Saturday, reflect on some ancient Hebrew honeymoon customs— Deuteronomy 20:5-7. On Sunday, finish up your study of marriage with a look at Proverbs 5:18.

FIVE MARRIAGE

DECISIONS

Making wise choices

I f the decision concerns what color sweater to wear, no big deal, right?
But what about if you have to select a college, or choose whether to go out
with a certain person, or pick where to work for the summer? In situations like
these, decision-making can be tricky.

Well, fret and sweat no more! Here's what God says about making wise choices.

"I have set before you life and death,
blessings and curses. Now
choose life, so that you
and your children may
live" (Deuteronomy
30:19).

L es is a smart, talented guy. He's also lazy.

Since Les wants to be an engineer, his dad recommended a challenging junior schedule of algebra, chemistry, history, English, computer programming, and physical education.

Les signed up for algebra, chorus, study hall, history, English, woodworking, and volleyball.

"Oh, so do you like to sing and work with wood, Les?"

"No. I signed up for those classes because they're an automatic A."

Don't just choose the easy road!

Look It Up: All too often, we adopt a lazy approach to life. Rather than seeking out challenges that will stretch us and cause us to grow, we choose easy options.

Thank God that Jesus didn't make His decisions based on which option was the easiest. Had He done that, we'd still be in our sins. Instead, His decision was to do God's will—no matter what.

"Jesus took the Twelve aside and told them, 'We are going up to Jerusalem, and everything that is written by the prophets about the Son of Man will be fulfilled. He will be handed over to the Gentiles. They will mock him, insult him, spit on him, flog him and kill him" (Luke 18:31-32).

Being murdered was not a fun plan. And yet Jesus' attitude was, "Father, if you are willing, take this cup from me; yet not my will, but yours be done" (Luke 22:42).

Think It Through: It doesn't seem like a big deal now, but Les made some poor academic choices last spring. He's having fun now, but when he goes off to college in the fall of '91, he'll kick himself for not having exposed himself to more courses relevant to engineering.

Are you making decisions now (spiritual, academic, social, physical) that may haunt you later?

Work It Out: Some "ABCs" for you:

Ask God to teach you this week how to make wise decisions.

Be sure to look up all the verses in the "Nail It Down" sections that follow.

Commit to a lifestyle of doing what is right, not just what is easy.

Nail It Down: See how wrong choices have lasting consequences—Judges 16.

?????????? O N E **DECISIONS** ???

It seemed so obvious. Abby had a clear choice between a job that paid $6 an hour and another one that paid only minimum wage.

After thinking about it for half a millisecond, she took the higher-paying job.

What a mistake! She has to work weird hours in a dark, smoke-filled office.

If she had picked the other job, she could have set her own schedule and worked with three friends in a bright, cheery atmosphere.

Look before you leap!

Look It Up: Some options can look really good . . . and turn out really bad:

"And quarreling arose between Abram's herdsmen and the herdsmen of Lot. The Canaanites and Perizzites were also living in the land at that time.

"So Abram said to Lot, 'Let's not have any quarreling between you and me, or between your herdsmen and mine, for we are brothers. Is not the whole land before you? Let's part company. If you go to the left, I'll go to the right; if you go to the right, I'll go to the left.'

"Lot looked up and saw that the whole plain of the Jordan was well watered, like the garden of the LORD, like the land of Egypt, toward Zoar. (This was before the LORD destroyed Sodom and Gomorrah.) So Lot chose for himself the whole plain of the Jordan and set out toward the east. The two men parted company: Abram lived in the land of Canaan, while Lot lived among the cities of the plain and pitched his tents near Sodom" (Genesis 13:7-12).

Think It Through: Lot's choice of land cost him dearly. He ended up in a gross place with gross neighbors. And he had even become a pretty gross person himself.

Has greed ever caused you to make a bad decision? How could Abby have avoided the wrong choice?

Work It Out: Are you facing a tough choice between two "good options"? Try the pro-con approach to decision-making. With the help of a parent, a youth leader, or a mature Christian friend, list all the positive and negative aspects to each of your possible choices.

Once you've done this, you may discover that one of your "good options" is not so good after all!

Nail It Down: Read Proverbs 18:15.

Pray About It:

? ? ? ? ? ? ? TWO

D ebbie is stunned. "Matt wants to ask me to his prom?"

"That's what he said."

"How excellent! I've been wanting to go out with Matt since early last summer."

"But what about your date with Donnie?"

"Kim, why would I go to a movie with Donnie when I could go to the prom with Matt?"

Three weeks later, Matt is finished with Debbie. And because of what she did to Donnie, so is everyone else.

When a little isn't enough . . .

Look It Up: When the Israelites demanded a king, the prophet Samuel spelled out the consequences of such a choice:

"He said, 'This is what the king who will reign over you will do: He will take your sons and make them serve. . . . He will take your daughters to be perfumers and cooks and bakers. He will take the best of your fields and vineyards and olive groves . . . . Your menservants and maidservants and the best of your cattle and donkeys he will take for his own use. He will take a tenth of your flocks, and you yourselves will become his slaves. When that day comes, you will cry out for relief from the king you have chosen, and the Lord will not answer you in that day.'

"But the people refused to listen to Samuel. 'No!' they said. 'We want a king over us. Then we will be like all the other nations, with a king to lead us and . . . fight our battles' " (1 Samuel 8:11, 13-14, 16-20).

Things happened just as Samuel said!

Think It Through: What did Debbie fail to consider when she broke her weekend date with Donnie?

Do you tend to think through the consequences of your choices before you make decisions?

Work It Out: Try the "Options & Consequences" method next time you face a big decision.

1. Identify the decision you are facing.
2. List all the options you could choose.
3. Ask God to help you see the possible consequences of each choice.
4. Select the option that results in the best, most biblical consequences.

Nail It Down: Read about how an angel of the Lord showed Joseph an option he had failed to consider— Matthew 1:18-25.

??????? THREE **DECISIONS** ???

A ndy is facing a really tough decision.

During the same week that the youth group has scheduled to host back-to-back Christmas parties for an orphanage and two nursing homes, a non-Christian friend has invited Andy to go snow skiing.

As a leader of his group, Andy feels responsible to be at the youth functions.

And yet, he remembers how much fun he had the only other time he went skiing. "Not only would I get to spend some time with Randy, but if I skied a whole week, I could really improve!"

? ? ? ? ? ?

FOUR

A checklist for choosing

Look It Up: The Apostle Paul's letter to the Corinthian Christians gives us practical advice for choosing wisely. Our decisions should result in actions that
• bring spiritual benefit to ourselves and others: "'Everything is permissible for me'—but not everything is beneficial" (1 Corinthians 6:12);
• help us spread the gospel (1 Corinthians 9:19-22);
• cause us to excel for Christ (1 Corinthians 9:25).
On the other hand, our choices should never
• lead us into enslaving habits (1 Corinthians 6:12);
• encourage another Christian to sin: "Therefore, if what I eat causes my brother to fall into sin, I will never eat meat again, so that I will not cause him to fall" (1 Corinthians 8:13);
• be selfish: "Nobody should seek his own good, but the good of others" (1 Corinthians 10:24).

Think It Through: Put yourself in Andy's shoes. How do you think you might feel? What do you think you'd actually decide to do? Why?
Can you think of any other Biblical criteria for making wise choices in life's gray areas?

Work It Out: Here are some other practical suggestions for making good decisions when the Bible doesn't spell out what you should do:
1. Pray, confidently expecting God to give you guidance (James 1:5-8).
2. Get as much wise counsel from as many wise Christians as you know (Proverbs 20:5, 18).
3. Explore God's Word for timeless principles that might apply to your specific situation.

Nail It Down: Read about the ultimate criterion for any choice we face—1 Corinthians 10:31.

Pray About It:

Andy—our friend from yesterday's story—finally made his decision this morning. After a lot of prayer and thought, he decided to turn down the invitation to snow ski with his friend Randy.

"After I searched my motives, and remembered some commitments I made this fall, I was pretty sure what I needed to do. Then, when I asked myself, 'What would Jesus do in this situation?' everything became crystal clear.

"I'm looking forward to the youth group projects."

What would Jesus do?

Look It Up: Perhaps the best way to figure out what Jesus would want you to do, is to look at how He made His decisions.

"Jesus gave them this answer: 'I tell you the truth, the Son can do nothing by himself; he can do only what he sees his Father doing, because whatever the Father does the Son also does. For the Father loves the Son and shows him all he does. Yes, to your amazement he will show him even greater things than these," (John 5:19-20).

His secret? Because of His close, moment-by-moment relationship to His Heavenly Father (and His commitment to do what was right) Jesus always made the right choices.

Think It Through: Remember this important fact: Deciding not to decide is, in reality, a decision!

Don't be afraid of making mistakes. If you have honestly and earnestly sought God's will through common sense, godly counsel, prayer, and the other methods we have discussed this week, you can be confident that you will make a wise choice.

Work It Out: For fun and relaxation during this holiday season, read the classic book *In His Steps* by Charles Sheldon. This best-selling novel focuses on some church members who decide to live their lives and make their daily decisions by first asking themselves the simple question, "What would Jesus do?"

Nail It Down: Read in 2 Timothy 2:15 about the most important decision a person can ever make. On Saturday, check out what the Bible says about motives in decision-making—Proverbs 21:2. Then on Sunday, read about a guy who tried (and failed) to avoid the responsibility of his own decision—Matthew 27:22-26.

????????? FIVE **DECISIONS** ????